j-fi Publishing

7620 Yonge Street

Thornhill , Ontario

L4J 1V9

National Library of Canada Cataloguing in Publications

Taylor, Randy

      Elevate/ Randy Taylor

Includes index.

ISBN 978-1-300-60984-1

     1.   Personal self-development

Production credits

Cover and design by Eye Q Designs

Printed in Canada

10 9 8 7 6 5 4 3 2 1

Contents

To my family

I never dared dream this big

Acknowledgments

Nothing happens in a vacuum. Sitting down and trying to thank all those who have been an integral part of my life and who have contributed to where I am today is a daunting task. I believe that every experience in life happens for a reason and that every person who touches your life is a destined part of the fabric.

From the early days, thanks to my guidance councilor Mr. Gretzinger whose encouragement and belief in me created a seed of what was possible. He was the man who after trying for over an hour to talk me out of leaving school left me with a statement that was the impetus for beginning to turn my life around. He said as I was walking out the door. *"Randy, I want you to know something. I want you to know where you are now has nothing to do with where you can go"*. That simple statement caused me to begin to question everything and to wonder if he was right. I discovered that he was. Not only for myself but for anyone.

A very large debt of gratitude is owed to my friend, Tom McArthur who was the one years ago posed the question *"So Randy, what do you want to do with your life?"* To which I answered, *"Since I was little I thought it would be amazing to be the guy on the radio"*. It was Tom who stood beside me that cold December day in my kitchen and encouraged me to make the call that would lead to a 20-year career in broadcasting. That giant leap made possible the discovering of my passion of pursuing this field of personal and professional development.

To my late mother for the happy times that I will always cherish and for your sense of humor and sense of wonder that I hope in some way I embody. To my siblings, Dennis and Don and Pat; for being there and doing you're best to shelter me from the storm when we were kids.

To my new family, Arnie and Ellie; thank you for entrusting your beautiful daughter to me, for believing in me and for making me so much of a part of the best family I have ever known. You are by far the richest people I have ever met. To Danny and Sara, Mathew, Alex and Ben and to Jamie and Laina, Shane and Drew, you add more color and substance to my life than you can know. A special hug for Laina who has been there for me every day trading encouragement for recipes. To Bubbi Elsie whose love and wisdom created a dynasty of great families and whose strength and character set the bar so high for us all to strive for in life.

It feels odd to thank my children because they are a gift that words can never begin to describe the blessing they bring everyday. To my son Justin who has been a light in my life for the past 34 years and who continues every day to be my inspiration and to his beautiful wife Sarah and son Jaden. To Myles whose talent, potential, sense of wonder and compassion fills me with love and makes me proud everyday. To Codi, whose beauty on the inside and out, bolstered by her free spirit allows me to love bigger and see what is possible. To Jonah, whose love and joy is overwhelming and who will forever be my heart song. Finally, to my little girl Faith. Your name has come forward in your spirit and you make my eyes shine every day. Because of you I have faith every day.

To everyone who has believed in me over the past 9 years of this journey into personal and professional development and to all who have entrusted your hopes and dreams to me through my coaching programs and seminars I owe you a debt of gratitude that I can't explain. Becoming a part of your lives and having the privilege to watch your dreams unfold has taught me more than you can know and created a joy that I could ever have imagined.

There is one person who I can't really find the words to thank. My best friend Alex Bril. It was you who opened doors I was not yet ready to walk though. You had an enormous impact on my life. It was your encouragement over coffee or a squash game or a bike ride that I will never forget. More than anything you made me believe. Not in who I was yet but who I could become. You are facing a challenge every day that none of us could understand and your strength and courage is a testament to who you have always been. A champion.

Finally, to my wife; My Joey. You are the living proof of destiny. From the day that we met I have been changed. I am in awe of everything you have done with your life and with ours. I have always been a dreamer and believed that anything was possible but this is bigger than even I could have imagined. As a wife, a partner, a very best friend and the most incredible mother possible to Jonah and Faith, you are more than I could have ever hoped for. Your love and support has made everything possible and every day a miracle. In every sense of the word you are my soul mate.

Introduction

"When someone dies the Greeks don't write obituaries.
They simply ask, did they have passion?"

I want you to consider the following very carefully. The absolute majority of people believe that where they are is where they are meant to be. I want you to know with everything that is inside of me that there is another way. What if this is your one moment in time? This exact moment when opportunity is knocking, announcing that you have the ability to change anything and everything. This one moment when you are faced with the real choice of what you can accomplish with your life. Will you set aside this opportunity to become and have and go anywhere and live with purpose and passion or will you turn away and commit the rest of your life to wondering what this is all about? Here is what you must know. In the 4 ½ billion years that this rock has been spinning out here and of the almost 7 billion people on earth today, there has never been a you and there never will be again. What are you going to do with it?

Something else to consider is that this very well may be the only time in your entire life when you make the commitment to dig down deep inside and draw out every ounce of intention and declare, *"I'm going to do this. I'm going to do whatever it takes to find out what I am truly capable of. I have decided that I am going to live my life with passion and purpose. I am capable of having the life that I want and need and crave. I will not stop until I have uncovered all that I am capable of and will continue on until I am living the life that I deserve. I am making a solemn promise to myself that I am not going to be one of those who are faced with the crushing question at the end of life, "What was this all about?" There is absolutely nothing I can't become and there is nothing that holds me to my current state. I have complete control over my destiny and I have the ability to change anything in this life that I choose. I will no longer look to just get through the day but I will get from the day. I am going to begin this process that will transform my life and become the person I am deserving of".*

Here is where we begin then; with a question. *"Do you love the life that you are living? Have you always wondered if you are capable of more"?* If the answer is yes, understand that you are not alone. One of the greatest psychological challenges today is to somehow connect with a knowing that our lives matter. That we count for something. That we in fact can live with purpose and passion and to know that we were created to leave our mark here. To know that our destiny is completely of our own choosing. You are completely unique and capable of becoming anything you set your mind to.

Sadly, the absolute majority has fallen into the trap of capitalism that states, *"If you trade your effort and give up tens of thousands of hours of your life, you will be given enough money to sustain yourself"*. Recent surveys have shown that 84% of people currently employed said they would be open to looking for a new job or employer this year. 70% of college graduates stated that the number one reason they attended was to earn more money. In effect they are trading life for money. There is another way.

So what is passion? Can you draw a picture of emotion? Describe it in terms so that another will feel what you feel? The simple truth is that it is not possible, yet emotion, passion specifically, is the greatest energy source of mankind. Passion has launched great wars, left footprints on the moon, sparked life for countless billions, created art and song and dance and has been responsible for almost every great achievement of our species. The unique thing about passion is this. It can only be felt by the individual.

I hated the hand I was dealt early on in life and now I am so grateful for it. I can't put into words just how fortunate I feel today. I was born into poverty and parent alcoholism and lived on the streets. Because of what happened to me and where I was I felt broken and incapable. Then I began to ask a question that changed everything. That question, *"But what if they're wrong. What if where I am now has nothing to do with where I can go?"* is what started the process and took me from where I was to where I am.

I discovered that this was not a question that only applied to me. It was true for anyone. I am now driven every day to help as many people as I can to own this question. To do this. To believe in themselves more than they do now. To take that belief and use it to create a life of passion and purpose. To know why they are here. To become all that they are capable of and to not arrive at the end of life wondering what this was all about.

I got away from where I was early on in life because I started to believe. Not in one cataclysmic explosion of belief but slowly over time. What happened was that one-day at a time this belief allowed me to travel all the way to normal. Normal being a regular lemming of society marching along, going to work each day, paying my bills, raising my family and wondering what this was all about. My belief had grown so much that I started to question everything. I started to search for what *I* really wanted out of life. I started to throw out the rules and dream bigger dreams. After all, the rules when I was young that said I would not amount to much were wrong and I began to wonder if just maybe these new rules were as well. Guess what. They were. As a result of the process of growing my belief, I was able to go from the streets to a job to the very top in broadcasting and now to lecturing and coaching some of the top leaders and corporations in the world.

I do what I do every day because I am driven to help you to drop kick these rules to the curb and to believe in yourself more. To just believe in yourself. To believe you can achieve anything you can imagine and live with passion. To believe you can grow your business. To believe you can improve your health and relationships and your ability to make a difference and change this world. That's why I do what I do. That's why I have dedicated my life's work to this and why I wrote this book. That is why I hope with ever ounce of my being that you do this. My ultimate goal is that this book is what causes you to head down the road of discovery and find what it is your heart beats for. Know that I will be waiting every day for the e-mail that will come from you proclaiming that you did it. That you are part of that growing trend of people who living an authentic life and achieving all they are capable of. The stories of the people I work with that end up in a place they never imagined are what provide the fuel for me every day.

While the choosing of the scenes from the movie of our lives is ultimately of our own choosing, the criteria for a life well lived is to live and have lived with passion. Today so many people are toiling and getting *"through"* life rather than getting from it. At 28 years old I walked away from a job I should have felt fortunate to have to start in radio part time at $4.25 an hour. At the time others thought I might be showing signs of instability. Those voices diminished over time and eventually I reached the very top in my field. At 47 when I turned the microphone off for the last time to jump off that cliff again to pursue this fantastic line of work, the term *"mid life crisis"* was bantered about. I sensed at the time that measurements were being taken to fit me for a white coat. To an outsider what I was doing looked absurd and out of reach. Looking back now I can say, of course it looked like that to them. They were not the one with passion. They were not driven as I was driven. They did not feel what I felt. Sadly, for most the very offering of logic from the naysayers of the world espousing all the reasons why this or that may not work, is what causes the flame of passion to flicker and go out. When the flame dies, with it goes the promise of living the life you were deserving and pushes you through the turnstile of the masses to simply trade life for money.

What this process is designed to do is to help you to go deep inside of yourself to discover your passion. The contrast of the life you are deserving of and the one you may be experiencing now will be more than you dreamed possible. Once you define your goals in life and find your passion, never expect the world to understand. They can't. Your passion and your emotionally connected goals are yours and yours alone.

One of the great traps society has laid is the notion that a sufficient amount of money equals success and happiness. I can tell you from the countless clients I have worked with over the years who for all intense and purpose have "made it", show up lost and broken and without purpose. I have had many sit in my office earning well over $1 million a year, who, when we begin talking about purpose and passion in life they get tears in their eyes. The truth is that the world is full of miserable rich people. What I am speaking of is not a repudiation of wealth. On the contrary we are all deserving of great wealth at the service of others while in the pursuit of our dreams. The caution I do have against wealth for wealth's sake is to ask *"what are we willing to pay for it"*? A great many of those who have achieved great wealth would tell you in a quiet moment that they paid too much. It cost them their sense of purpose and passion and wonder. Sadly it also cost them their health and family and community and legacy. The price they paid was too much.

Four great words that sum up what our goal in life should be, echo across the ages. Those words are etched in the pages of the American Constitution. They align the compass of our life's direction to grab hold of all that we are deserving of. Those words are, *"The pursuit of happiness"*. In the simplest terms that's really what this process is all about. To discover your true goals and passion. To live it. To understand that this is truly what the pursuit of happiness is all about. Many would have the question, *"Sure, but is this possible for me"*?

It is a fact that it is possible for every one of us to arrive at this destination. What I will also tell you from the outset is that this will not be easy. Gaining the ultimate prize in life never is. Everything that is worth having is worth working for. There will be challenges and setbacks. Sacrifices and doubt. Ask this question, *"What is the alternative"?* Consider for just a moment of what would it feel like one day at the end of your time here to realize that you never lived the life you were capable of? Coming to the sad realization that it's over and you never really tried.

Jim Rohn once said,

> *"We will all pay one of two pains in life. The pain of discipline*
> *is small. The pain of regret is huge".*

Make the decision to not pay the latter. It is *this* pain beyond all else that I am driven to help you avoid.

Getting from where you are to where you want to be will involve a process. One of the greatest gifts to come from my work coaching thousands of individuals over many years has been to learn in real time what steps are necessary to create real lasting change that can make anything possible for you. Possible for anyone.

The first step in discovering your own passion and vision in life is to begin first by tracing back your journey of how you got here. It is not possible to make the necessary steps to go *"there"* if we don't first understand how we got *"here"*. There is a core process of success that is true for us all. This is a question that I pose to every audience I speak to. *"If you set a goal, find out what is necessary to achieve it, begin to invest in the activity and you don't stop any goal in life is possible".* Every single time with every person in the audience the answer is a resounding yes. That is an absolute. What stops us is what I now know to be the greatest nemesis to mankind. It is the voice in our head that is constantly challenging everything that we desire. This *"voice"* is not something that we are born with. It is a voice created from hundreds of thousands of impressions from the world around us through personal experience. This *"voice"* is responsible for implanting the doubt into our minds. It is the subversion of our belief that creates the greatest challenge and in the end is responsible for countless millions not achieving what they were capable of or living the lives they deserved. It is not possible to win the war if you first don't understand the enemy. You will come to know that the great dream slayer that has beaten you back thus far is nothing more than a thought.

If you already know what your passion in life is, you will have succeeded in taking the first giant step towards living an authentic life. If you don't know what it is, this process will help you uncover it. It is of critical importance to know this. Living a life of passion and connecting to our own authentic goals is not something that is possible for some. Passion is inside of each and every one of us. Here is what I know for sure. It's inside of *you*. Passion after all is the foundation of life itself and the magic elixir that provides the energy that makes everything possible. One of the pitfalls of the way our society is structured is that almost everything we do in life is related, equated and cross-referenced with our "job". That three letter word is responsible in a very large way to causing the disconnect from living with passion for the majority.

Passion is not a job you see. Passion is a *"love of"*. Passion is a love of people or numbers, animals or technology, travel or health, children or philanthropy, storytelling, art or song or dance. Passion is the expression of the emotion that is evoked when partaking in what your heart beats for. A *"job"* is merely the societal capitalistic structure that allows us to derive income from the exchange of goods and services while engaging in what we love. Why not allow your job to sustain you while engaged in the pursuit of happiness? It makes me smile to think back to the last time I had a "job". It was 29 years ago. Prior to that I was one of those who kept trading life for money, moving from one employer to another in search of an answer that would create the emotion. I kept hoping that the change of scenery or an increase in salary or a new boss would be the magic pill I was looking for that would light my fire of passion.

29 years ago I embarked on a journey into the world of entertainment through radio and television. For 20 years I loved every minute of it and as a result it was never work. 9 years ago I turned off the microphone for the last time and left to do this. That move allowed me to push the passion meter even higher to involve my life in this most fascinating world of helping others achieve their dreams. Here is what I can tell you with total certainty. I have not worked a day in the past 29 years. I should also note that I was able to do all this with only a grade 10 education.

Along the path towards personal fulfillment and living a life of passion there will be changes you will likely need to make that will allow for this transformation. Nothing is as simple as *"there it is"* now go and get it. You are likely aware of the phenomenon of the book and documentary from a few years back called The Secret. It of course detailed the philosophy behind the Law of Attraction. Many people were initially drawn in, fascinated and motivated by it. The law of attraction is absolute. The book and documentary however oversimplified it to a point of distraction. Esther Hicks who was in the original version and then pulled out early on over the media over-hype, clarified what it takes to use the law of attraction I think better than I have ever heard it put. She said, *"It would be easier to be hearing these words* (the philosophy of the law of attraction) *if they had come to you on your first day of life experience but they are not. You've been here for a while".* Ah, there lies the true answer. We've been here for a while. The *"been here for a while"* has allowed for the intake of tens of thousands of hours of audio and video from the world around us. This information and the experiences we have all had have done two things. They have filled the sub-conscious mind with great information we can make use of. They have also filled our heads with a great deal of psychological baggage that we carry around with us everyday. This baggage in effect is the voice we hear inside of our heads every day, all day long.

This voice natters on as to why this won't work, or why this is too hard or why we don't have what it takes to lead the life we are deserving of or have always wanted. The great news is that there is tremendous science behind human behavior, detailing the intake and storage of information, how it affects our current and future decisions and how it can be altered to serve us rather than tear us down. There is also an incredibly strong chemically addictive process linking emotions to behavior that must be controlled if we are to gain dominion over our lives. We will talk in great detail of this behavioral science and how to use it to our advantage. In the end the most powerful component of true authentic success comes down to three words. They are, *"Belief, belief, belief".*

Once you have uncovered your passion and vision in life the real work starts of how to breathe life into it. The belief we just spoke of will be tested in ways you can't possibly know at this moment. One of the greatest tools you will need to overcome the challenge of *"the voice"* will be a well laid out map of how you plan on going from where you are to where you want and deserve to be. The primary positioning statement from the latest coaching program I developed (Breakthrough Coach) is this. *"The difference between wanting and having is doing"*. In the simplest terms you are here and you will want to be there. Getting there will involve devising a plan, taking the first step and then investing the will and skill to continue doing what is necessary. As we discussed earlier any goal is possible by implementing this simple philosophy, *"Set the goal, find out what is necessary to achieve it, begin to invest in the activity and then don't stop"*. Again, great detail and attention will need to be paid to the planning of this journey. There are two paths we will discuss in detail. They are the cliff or the bridge. The cliff being an abrupt change in what you are doing. The bridge will involve utilizing your current situation to allow for the change and transition to take place over time. It is important to know that both options are available to us all. Twice I choose the cliff. Looking back now it may have been an easier journey if I had started off by using a bridge. You will ultimately be the one who decides which direction to take once you have identified your passion.

We will also discuss and implement proven processes that will allow you to become a master at relationships, develop discipline and structure, improve focus, implement an entirely new approach to business development and grow and improve in all areas of life. Success without balance is a hollow victory.

As the great quote by Lau Tsu stated, *"The journey of a thousand miles begins with the first step"*. Nothing is possible without first a beginning. What we are not told in that quote is that we must keep walking. Taking that first step off the cliff or across the bridge can be empowering and exhilarating and frightening. Before long however the reality of the length of your journey will set in and your goal, which could be far off in the distance may appear stationary. As a result, if we don't fully understand the psychological properties of the necessity of incremental growth, it will become increasingly more difficult to continue with the activity required. Without this, the voice in your head will in all likelihood win the day and convince you to stop walking long before you arrive at your destination. It is the stopping that has littered the pages of history with the broken dreams of the masses. Not that all dreams were not possible, they were. It was just that those who failed stopped. They stopped short of doing what was necessary to achieve the life they were deserving of and to grab hold of that brass ring of life.

Finally we will teach you life's great rule of success. This rule is the most basic and perhaps the most powerful of all that will allow you move from living the life you are to the one you are deserving of. This entire process will begin with the tiniest of sparks. That spark will give off a wisp of smoke until a small flame begins to take hold. Guard well the flame from the thieves that surround us everyday lest it be blown out and with it the promise of a life lived with passion.

The last point I would like to make is an appeal really. This is a book but I made the decision that I didn't want it to be that. I truly am not writing this to put the term "Author" on my business card or to simply take up another of the spots on your bookshelf. I want you to use it. To invest in the time and energy necessary through all aspects of growth to arrive at the place where you belong. I am a collector of great stories. I will be waiting for yours. What drives me to write these words is the hope that one day soon you will send me your story of where you are and what you have achieved and become. Know that I will be waiting.

We will begin first with the telling of a story. It is the story of why so many get lost on their journey of personal fulfillment. It's an illustration of the understanding of where your true magic lies.

The Magic Pill

T he flame from the oil lamp flickered, casting shadows over the interior of the cabin. Hand hewn beams, stained and discolored from years of smoke framed the bleak living quarters. The air was acrid and heavy. Any communication or human connection had abandoned this place long ago. This was where he had labored for the past 9 years, 3 months and four days.

Rafael sat crouched at his bench surrounded by glass jars filled with foul smelling substances. Only the stark necessities of life were evident. A straw mattress in the corner. A wood stove and worktable, long scarred from the preparation of meager meals and thousands of experiments. Stacks of hand written journals lay claim to the failed formulas of yesterday. Food was brought in only once a month and water was offered up by the rain or from the stream that wandered through the forest down the hill. Sustenance, sleep and contact with the outside world were all seen as wasted distractions.

For all these days. For all these months. For all these years he had banished himself into seclusion in search of what he was certain must be. The formula that would provide all the wealth the world had to offer.

The health and everlasting life that would spring from the secret formula he was so certain he could create. He was after all an alchemist. It was his raw belief that pushed him on to unearth the formula. The magic pill. During these past weeks his search had grown somewhat frantic.

The morning light of the next day filtered in through the grime-coated windowpanes, casting an eerie pallor over his bed and he began to stir. Dust particles hung suspended in the air, illuminating the shards of light that crept across the floor, spreading out into the dark corners of the cabin. As the mental fog began to lift from his sleep, he became aware of his body and his breathing. The usual anticipation of a new day was not there. He had no energy. The flame that had burned inside all these years on this journey was flickering low. With all he had, Raphael summoned what little strength he had to push himself up on the straw mattress and lean against the cabin wall. His breath rattled inside his chest. His mind blurred and the room spun out of focus from just this simple shift. He could feel that something was different this morning. Something very wrong.

After a few moments his vision began to clear and he cast a glance around the cabin. He sensed there was no strength in him to move from this spot in the corner. What was wrong? Would this feeling pass? Would he be able to get up one more time and go on with his day. With his experiments? With his search?

Summoning more strength he closed his eyes for a moment and tried to focus. When he opened them he was startled and his heart began to race.

Sitting before him on the floor was a man draped in a shimmering cloth robe. Long white hair framed his face. His eyes, dark pools of calm appeared to draw him in. They were the eyes of wisdom and experience. A light appeared to radiate from his skin, casting a glow in the space around him. Sensing that he must be in a dream Raphael spoke, believing this would bring him back.

"Who are you?" he asked

"I am the messenger" replied the man.

The voice was low and soothing. He began to become aware that this was not a dream but in spite of that his trepidation began to subside and his heartbeat slowed. There was great peace in the eyes of the man who sat before him.

"How did you get in here? What do you want?" he asked.

"I am here because it is time. I was sent for you Raphael" the man said.

"Time? Time for what? Who sent you?" he asked, his voice becoming more demanding.

"It is time for you to leave this place. Your time here has come to an end." He said

"Bbb...but this is my cabin". He stammered *"This is my home. This is where I must continue my work. All of my tools are here. You can't ask me to leave"* he pleaded, *"I have done no wrong"*

"No, I am not telling you that you must leave this cabin. I am here to tell you that it is time to leave this world. Your time here has come to an end" he said with a certainty and calm that left little doubt.

"I am dying? Is that what you are telling me, that I am dying?" he asked.

"Yes, as that is your word for it. Yes, you are dying and this will be your final day here." The stranger replied.

"But why? Why now? How could this happen?" Raphael begged. *"I have worked so long and tried so hard to find the formula. I know if I had just a bit more time I will find it. The formula that will breathe life and strength back into my body. The formula that will provide all that I have ever wanted"* he said.

"If you had another ten thousand years my friend you would not find it. You have been looking in the wrong place all along. You have searched everywhere but where it has always been".

"Where? He asked.

"Inside of you. It's been there all along" the messenger replied.

"What has?"

"The formula you dedicated your life's work to finding. This magic pill as you have called it. The formula for all that you sought was hidden inside of you; for health and happiness and wealth and peace. You have always had it. Neither you nor any other could break this code from the outside. This formula requires millions of ingredients and trillions of processes to complete. The calculations are beyond your comprehension and will always be. There has always been just a single method for the creation of what you desire. That is to learn that you have dominion over your body and can connect your mind to your heart. To your true heart and passion of your purpose on this earth and to direct your spirit to move beyond the confines of your physical body" he answered.

"I don't understand. If this was inside of me all along, why was I not able to see it? Why did I not know this and find it before now?" he asked

"It is not your fault Raphael. This search has been engrained in your culture. In the generations that came before you and those who will come after. Since you were a little boy you have been made to believe that the answer was out there for what you desired if only you looked hard enough." He replied.

"Can I still find the formula if I start to look inside?"

"No, I am afraid that your days have passed."

"But what did I miss? What should I have known?"

"That your body was designed for perfection. That all you needed to function perfectly lies inside of you. To grow and to heal and to transport you effortlessly anywhere you wanted to go. To take you everywhere and anywhere you desire. To give you the very power of creation to produce life itself so that a part of you could live on." He answered with a calm assurance.

"But why do I learn this only now. For what purpose then was my life?" Raphael asked in a forlorn tone.

"To leave this knowledge as your legacy. That is your purpose Raphael. This is the formula of life. To know that all you need to control your mind and create all that is possible is inside. To know that your body is yours and is subject to your will where you can access the formula to create perfect health. To know that you are much more than your physical body; that your spirit travels out into the world and is connected to everything. The formula to create all that you could comprehend lies inside of you. It has always been there"

Raphael's mind raced. As he began to form another question the light emanating from the messenger began to grow brighter and brighter until his features and most of his shape were no longer visible. For a moment the light was so intense it illuminated the entire inside of the cabin. Then, within moments it began to dissipate. The light dimmed and faded until it was gone completely. When his eyes adjusted once again to the dim light of the room the messenger was no longer with him. He was alone once again.

For a moment Raphael sat in silence contemplating what has just happened. On the floor beside his bed rested his journal opened to the last entry of the experiment from the day before. Willing himself with every bit of his strength he reached out, picked it up and placed it upon his lap. Grasping a pen in his trembling hand he thought long about what to record here. Finally, he steadied himself and wrote,

"I have found it. My search is over. It is inside. Look inside. The formula lies there"

The pen dropped from his fingers onto the page and he rested his head back against the cabin wall and closed his eyes. He could feel his energy begin to slip away. Within moments his breathing slowed and the world faded to black. His time had come. The life force was leaving his body. His journey here had come to an end.

This is the story that has played out for the multitudes over the centuries. This is the story of mankind and the search for the magic pill. The magic you see is inside of you. It has always been there.

1

What is Passion?

e begin with this question. *"What is passion?"* After all, we can't move towards what we can't identify. Passion is the foundation and the first building block in the creation of everything meaningful. Passion has nothing to do with logic or reason. Passion is the manifestation of positive energy brought about through the engagement in activity or thought that creates positive emotion. Passion is not a job although you may derive passion from your work. Passion at its core level is a *"love of"*. Passion when first identified is a love of animals or technology. People or numbers. The cosmos or music or art or creation. Passion is a love of writing, story telling, children, nature, food or travel. Passion is quite simply being able to articulate the statement coming from your heart that says, *"I love this"*. Most importantly passion is 100% individual. Most get faked out into thinking that passion begins with a job. That's where most get lost while in the search for what their heart beats form. A job you see is simply the final element in the process whereas you are enabled to engage in your passion and take your efforts and skills to the marketplace. A job is merely the vehicle to provide for monetary rewards to sustain you while engaged in the active participation of your passion.

The seeds of passion are cast in our DNA. There is no real rhyme or reason why I am passionate about this and you of that. What happens throughout our lives is as we age we are told again and again that we will discover our calling or passion in life. *"This is something that comes with maturity"* we are reminded over and over again. The truth is that passion is something that for most begins at a very early age. The tragedy is that as we grow older the world beats it out of us and we are told to direct our focus towards being responsible and earn a good living. There is nothing logical or responsible about passion. It is an emotion plain and simple.

I was reminded of this story from the words written on the pages of a book given to me as a birthday present from my father-in-law. Those words reinforced my core belief of the process. The book is called *"The Last Lecture"*. You have likely heard of the story of the young professor who, when faced with certain death from pancreatic cancer decided to do for real what most professors pontificate on during their careers. It is called *"The last lecture"*. The premise being, that if you had only one lecture left to give, what would it be? *"What wisdom would you impart on the world if you knew this was your last chance and what would you want your legacy to be?"*

In his case, a very powerful premise given that for the professor and father of three little boys the weight of his words are palpable. Near the end of the first chapter titled, *"An Injured Lion Still Wants to Roar"* he was able to articulate what his decision was of what his last lecture was going to be about. Here is what he wrote,

"It came to me in a flash. Whatever my accomplishments, all of the things I loved were rooted in the dreams and goals I had as a child....and in the ways I had managed to fulfill almost all of them. My uniqueness, I realized, came in the specifics of all of the dreams- from incredibly meaningful to decidedly quirky-that defined my forty-six years of life. I've decided to call the lecture, "Really achieving your childhood dreams".

When I read those words they spoke so clearly of my belief. Words that are still here, surviving the writer himself. Words that sum up what I have always believed. That the dreams we have as a child, while covered up and painted over, still offer the greatest opportunity to peer into our own soul and find out what makes us tick. Those dreams are still there. Go looking. You will find them there, at the bottom of the trunk waiting to be dusted of and to have life breathed into them once again. We were all born you see with these seeds of passion.

What I am asking you to do throughout this process is to go in search of your own passion on purpose. This is what drives me everyday. To reach out to anyone I can and tell them that they can do the work to find it on purpose. I know and believe that living with passion is not just for some but for all. I was one of the lucky ones a great many years ago that tripped over it. The stars all aligned in just the right way for me to begin the process to do what I was passionate about. That shift has allowed me to live with passion for the past 29 years. I am now driven each and every day to help as many people as humanly possible to go in search of it and to find it on purpose.

This process of discovering your passion and connecting to your "why" is rooted in honesty. It's fascinating to consider that since we are old enough to begin to communicate we are told over and over again that the virtue of honesty is one of the cornerstones of life and a quality that must be adhered to and espoused if we are to live a good life and be treated as we would like to be treated. It's of critical importance to note that with all this focus on honesty we are rarely reminded of the virtue of being honest with ourselves. What we focus on and repeat becomes engrained into the subconscious mind, which then becomes the lead director in our lives. We will cover this in great detail in chapter 4 on the science of human behavior as to why this is so. The constant reminder of honesty in our dealings with others is what is responsible for the development of great character. The lack of this reminder of being honest with ourselves has the exact opposite affect. You find it difficult to be honest with yourself because it has not achieved the same attention as the latter. This conditioning is responsible for us often questioning our honesty with others and rarely with ourselves. The question then, *"Are you living the life you believe you are deserving of?"* rarely gets asked.

A few years ago I heard someone frame the entire journey in just a few words. I was watching an interview with U.S. General Russell Honoré who had been put in charge of the relief efforts in New Orleans during hurricane Katrina a number of years earlier. They were talking about life and goals and dreams when the general turned to the interviewer and said, *"There are only 2 important days in any person's life. The day you are born and the day you get to figure out why"*. Do this. Commit to this. Do whatever it takes to be the person who gets to find out why and who lives not a good life but a great one. Don't stop until you get to figure out your why.

One of the key points I would like to make it to not confuse your current goals with your passion. Finding what our heart beats for can be tricky business. Very often when speaking to groups on this topic I ask the audience if they have goals. When I ask nearly every hand goes up in the room. *"Yes, or course I have goals"* is the standard response. On occasion I have then told them that we are going to take 10 minutes and I want everyone to get out a piece of paper and write down their goals. After which I select a few people and go off and meet with them individually. Looking at the list I comment, *"This looks like a good list. These look like good goals, but let me ask you. Do you wake up in the morning driven and inspired to achieve what you have written down"?* Almost every person asked would say, *"I'm not and I don't know why"*, to which I reply, *"I do, they are not your goals"*. If the goals you have do not create positive emotion and inspire you and push you to do what is necessary when you wake up in the morning they are not your goals. They are the goals the world has given you. Over a lifetime through hundreds of thousands of impressions we are told that we should want *this* and become *that* and go *there*. This conditioning of the subconscious mind over time creates a belief that these are your goals. The fact remains that if there is no emotional connection to these goals then clearly they are not your own. The process of discovering what moves you will involve going inside and stripping away what the world has told you to want and to uncover what you want for you. Goals that you are connected to and inspired by. Jim Rohn once said, *"If you choose to build a cabin in the woods and feed the squirrels and you pull it off then you are a smashing success"*. To which the world would reply, *"But you're feeding squirrels"*. The answer to their challenge then is this, *"But you have no idea how that makes me feel"*. Again, discovering your passion is not about logic, it's about emotion.

What happens along the journey towards becoming what our heart beats for happens to us all. I often tell the story in seminars of an interview I watched a while back on Larry King. Larry was interviewing a Pastor and they were talking about the constant challenges President Obama was facing. Regardless of what good he was doing he remained under constant attack over those things he had not yet done or what was not going well. Larry asked the pastor how he could deal with such opposition. The pastor said, *"One thing I would like the president and everyone watching to understand about overcoming challenge. That is that faith does not mean the absence of doubt"*. Truer words were never spoken. It is something we all must accept and come to terms with. No matter how great our desire. No matter how much progress is made. No matter how far we have travelled we must all understand this. *Faith does not mean the absence of doubt.* You see faith and doubt live in the same house. Accept that as faith and passion and desire moves us forward, doubt will always be there challenging all that we long for and are deserving of. Doubt is that voice in our head that challenges every thought and every move and every action. It is also critically important to know this. Doubt is merely thought. It is not real. It presents no physical barrier of psychological challenge so insurmountable that can't be overcome. Accept that doubt will always be there but will diminish and get quieter over time. We must accept that the volume may diminish but will never go away completely. When you hear the doubt, know that it can only affect our progress if you allow it to. Do this and you will be well on your way to mounting the offensive that will ultimately lead to victory.

What I want to do in the following pages is to share with you some of the writing I have done over the years as it pertains to passion. Each day I write a piece called *"Perspectives"* on personal and professional development that goes out to my clients. Perspectives are a daily account of average ordinary life experiences and what the life lessons are from them. One of the topics I often write about is passion. The collection of these writings is in the process of being released as a book. It is my hope that from these stories selected, you will be able to gain a clear understanding of passion as it relates to every day life.

Perspectives:

A philosophy that stands the test of time

There are certain events in all of our lives that touch us and leave a lasting impression. Sometimes scars form. Other times fond memories take their place in the album of our lives. Still others have the capacity to imprint on our psyche and personal philosophy. One day a memory of mine came to the fore with blinding clarity that began to stir an interest in politics. It stirred an awakening belief in just what may be possible. The passing of Senator Edward Kennedy took me back to a hospital bed in early June 1968. I was 13 at the time and was hospitalized to have my appendix removed. On the second day after surgery the funeral of Bobby Kennedy was broadcast on every television channel available. The world had not yet healed from the loss of his brother, President John F Kennedy and here we were thrust into another unspeakable event. A small black and white television hung suspended over my bed on a mechanical arm. Mine was one of few rooms with a television. I'm not sure why I had it because we certainly couldn't afford it. That afternoon as the funeral was televised, no less than five nurses sat on the corners of my bed watching the service. Ted Kennedy read the eulogy as the camera panned back from the casket, through the back of the church and out the doors. It continued to pull back over the reflecting pool and the Washington Monument. His words were powerful. Wrought with emotion and eloquence. It was the final statement that I have always remembered. His closing words echoed the quote of George Bernard Shaw. He said, *"Some men see things as they are and ask why. My brother saw things that never were and asked why not"*. As the last words trailed off I looked around at the nurses on my bed. All of them, grown women were weeping openly. I felt the tears running down my own face before I was even aware that I was crying. Beyond the sadness I heard the message. It was a message that said more is possible. It was a message that I needed to hear and have never forgotten. Take heed of those words and the potential in your own life. Adopt it as your own when embarking on a new journey or stretching the bounds of your own belief and imagination. Do this then. *"See things that never were and ask why not"*. This is one philosophy that stands the test of time.

Perspectives:

Where you are today does not equal tomorrow

H ere is what we have the chance to do right now. At this very moment. This is not something to put on our to do list or file it in the "soon" category but *now*. Right this very moment.

We have the capacity to make the decision, to steel ourselves to say *"now"* is when I choose to stop putting it off. *Now* is the time I will commit to bringing real change to my life; to doing the things I know will move me closer to the life I deserve.

I could write on and on about the potential loss of tomorrow or the tragedy of a missed opportunity but I won't. I don't believe I need to. I know it well and can see this so clearly for myself and know you can too.

Most of us are presented with a limited number of opportunities to go for it. To really go after life and live it to the absolute best of our ability. This is one of those times. I want this to be one of those opportunities. Don't allow today to be one of those days you look back on and say *"I wish I would have tried"*. Set the goal to live your life so that you will one day reflect on *"I did it all and loved every moment of it "*.

Perspectives:

What is possible for you?

What I love to do is stand back and watch the reaction when I ask this question. *"What are truly you capable of during your time here on earth"? Not can I earn double my salary or have a nicer home but all of it. What are you truly capable of becoming"?* It is usually the first question I ask of all audiences I speak to. I think it is one of the great questions of life and remarkably one almost no one takes the time to ask.

As we spin about in a communication driven world, fuelled by the internet and face book; CNN and Facebook; Instant messaging, texting and video conferencing, this one little question gets lost in the frantic pace of life. I want you to take a moment and really consider it. Isn't finding the answer to this what life is supposed to be all about?

My own struggle with this question early on in life came in fits and starts. I have been asked many, many times if there was an event or a person or moment that created the impetus to go from where I was to where I am. I finally realized after many years that for me, making it to normal was the greatest distance I will likely ever travel and the most enlightening. Normal was having a job and a home and food on the table and the feeling that I belonged. I finally belonged. Once I realized that I could go make it to normal, the thought of the next goal or climbing the next hill appeared not only possible but also likely.

It is astounding to think that the vast majority of our fellow human beings will go through 60,70,80, 90 years or more and never stop long enough to really ask this question. Not simply, *"Can I make more money or have a bigger car or get the corner office, but all of it"*. I want you to be in the minority. For some reason that you and I may never know, you have been brought to this place where you are being faced with the question. Ask it. Ask it now. Ask it tonight. Ask it tomorrow and keep asking every day until you get the answer. *"What is really possible for me?"* I expect the answer is more than you could have ever imagined.

Perspectives:

When you believe.

All that we do and all that we accomplish and all that is possible is linked to whether or not we believe. One night after dinner we were cleaning up the dishes and my son Jonah (he was 4 at the time) asked about a toy and whether it would be possible to get it for Christmas.

My wife, thinking quickly said, *"We know a few things that you are getting for Christmas you know. Your daddy called the North Pole today and talked to Santa"*. With that his eyes went wide and a big smile crossed his face. *"Really"*? he exclaimed. *"Daddy talked to Santa? I bet he's going to come to my house first"*. There is no question in his mind that this mystical figure will live up to the legend and fill his stocking and his wish list on Christmas morning. Fascinating to see how strong his belief was and how powerful it can be. His belief so far has allowed him to become skilled in some rather challenging areas. He believed he could sit up and he did. He believed he could walk and he did. He believed he could learn the most difficult language in the world and with seemingly little effort and he did. When searching for the gifts and skills that will propel us to achieve all that we see in our minds eye, look no further than the nearest child. Learn to believe as they do. Re-learn to believe as they believe. And as Christmas Eve falls upon us, look up to the sky. You never know. He just may come to your house first. It's all possible when you believe.

Perspectives:

Anything is possible when you have faith.

We often reflect on the perceived challenges in life and question the possibility of our hopes and goals and dreams. It is this very questioning of what is possible that creates the greatest obstacle we will likely ever face. At 1:45 on a Friday morning, my Faith was strengthened and will unquestionably impact my life in the coming years in ways I can't yet comprehend. Faith for me is no longer just an ethereal psychological commitment. Faith is now my daughter. Faith Ella to be exact. I won't gush, but if we do meet up, know that I have pictures. She made her entry into this world lightly tipping the scales at 6 pounds, 7 ounces. You are no doubt thinking that it makes sense that I would name my daughter Faith, given what I do everyday. The truth is that the name

Faith was chosen by her mother more than 20 years ago. This little girl, broke a stalwart chain of 6 boys in a row to become the first and only girl on my wife's side. The enormous leap of faith that it took to bring her mom and I together still feels surreal. To detail every aspect of faith that was required to bring me to this point in time would fill a modest library.

I sat with my sister-in-law, Laina that night after visiting hours were over, talking about all of this and here is what came of it. We took note of how fascinating it is that no matter how often faith is rewarded, we return again and again to the well of despair and question the legitimacy of one more goal or one more step up the mountain. I can't question it ever again. It may seem quirky, but there is a stork on my front lawn proclaiming the arrival of *"Faith"* into this world on March 20th, the first day of spring. This simple proclamation and her pending impact on this world over the next one hundred years or so has burned it crystal clear into my mind of just what is possible. What is possible for her and for me and for you and for everyone. For all of it. This is all you need know. Anything is possible when you have Faith.

Perspectives:

Who are the flowers for anyway?

F or the closet gardeners out there, there is always that initial sense of it being just the right weekend to get the jump start on spring planting. It is interesting to watch what happens on your own street. It's a microcosm of the world and how the ebbs and flows of life can be viewed. We moved onto this street two and a half years ago and it appears that there has been a bustle of activity since. Young families growing.

Renovations, landscaping, new cars and new seasons. I was outside most of the weekend, engaging in one of those things that I love. Gardening and landscaping. When we bought the house it was rundown and overgrown and you could hardly see it from the street. Now the overgrown shrubs and tired lawn has been replaced with new sod and shrubs and flowers and life. Each season allows me to coax a new garden bed to take hold or a new perennial to find its home.

We have the best neighbours and have gotten to know most of them on a first name basis. My escapades with the house and yard have brought out more than a few good natured comments. My one neighbour has begged me to stop working on the yard. Laughingly he tells me that every time I do something new, his wife gets on him to do something to their home. We all do it don't we? It used to be called *"Keeping up with the Jones's"* . While out planting and raking and watering that phrase played out in my mind over and over. *"Keeping up with the Jones's"*. It is the quintessential example of the voice of society pushing us to do something that may not be from our own authentic wish list. The truth is that we only get one life to live and it would be a shame if we were doing what we are doing simply to compete with another. Check in with yourself often and ask the question, *"Who am I doing this for?"*

I asked this question of myself several times over the weekend. The answer was me. For a great many years I wondered and imagined what it would be like to have a lawn of my own to fuss over. Now I know. The flowers were for me. That's the lesson I guess. Make certain that whatever you plant is for you and not for what the world will think of you.

Perspectives:

What would you do with $48. Million?

A great many people love to play the lottery game. The commercial on the radio one day pegged the prize at $48 million. There is great truth and personal philosophy involved in the winning of a lottery. The mere thought of winning allows us to see for ourselves what we would do if we were to win. Designing our lives and connecting to our passion involves much the same process. Here is what winning the lottery does. It removes all the obstacles, first and foremost the psychological ones. Think about how clearly your life would unfold before your eyes if I were to hand you the winning ticket. The places you would go. The home you would live in. The people you would help and most importantly what you would choose to do with your time. Would you paint or sing, fish or write, travel or read, spend time with family or just spend time with yourself?

This is a great lesson and you don't have to win the lottery to design your own life and discover your passion. Do this. Go inside and look for those same thoughts brought to life by this "*roll of the dice pile of money*". If you do this and truly connect to what matters in your life, the money will not matter. As a matter of fact, when most find their passion and direction in life, the money ends up showing up as a bi-product of a life lived on purpose. What would you do with $48 million? What if I told you that with what you have inside right now you already won? You have you know.

Perspectives:

The true measure of success

Here's the goal in this business of personal growth. In the simplest terms what this is about is to try and help others to get it right. There is no one perfect formula to this end but I think there are some guideposts. To live your life at the service of others. To be authentic. To count for something. To leave this place better off than when we found it. Sadly I had to attend the funeral of a client and friend who left us much too soon. That part of the story I will leave to those much more learned than I. I don't know why some get a century while others less than half. What I do know is the life we gathered to mourn and to celebrate today was measured in terms that were real. The words of all who spoke at the service told of her caring nature. Love of life. Value as a parent, friend, co-worker. She was someone others had learned to count on and were never let down over decades. There was no mention of the size of her home, the make of her car or the depth of her bank account. I don't want this to come across as a repudiation of all material possessions because it is a fine goal to provide for yourself and your family from the fruits of your labour at the service of others. I was just struck by how simple and basic and real this life was measured and by all accounts along with her family, this world is the one who will suffer by her passing. There is an old Cherokee Proverb that says this "*When you were born, you cried and the world rejoiced. Live your life so that when you die, the world cries and you rejoice*". There is an entire philosophy of life in those simple 23 words. Take a moment and think about them and your own journey here. When your time here is up, what would you have the world cry for?

Perspectives:

Hey, where are you going?

There is a very well worn path that society has trampled down over the centuries. This is the path we are encouraged and even expected to walk along. Deviating too far from it can make you an outcast and the object of ridicule. This was one of those rare days when moving counter to the flow of the river is not only encouraged but planned. It has been called backwards day. This is not some governmental deficit reduction program, it's just a fun day that my son gets to take part in. He is in junior kindergarten. Amazing to see how engrained the concept of conformity has become even at this age. The thought of the logo on your t-shirt being on the back or the zipper in your pants being worn on the opposite side of your body is totally outrageous. Even at the ripe old age of four this structure has become firmly ensconced into his psyche. Logos go here and zippers go there. Baseball caps face this way and walking is only done in this direction. Little wonder when we dare to be so bold as to actually challenge the status quo that we face an onslaught of opinionated input. *"How could you live there? You can't make a living at that! We don't raise our children that way. You should get a real job. What makes you think you could actually become that"?* The truth is that being able to accomplish what we set out to do is not the challenge. The real test comes when we choose not to walk down the road that society travels. Know this. Backwards day is not just for 4 year olds in kindergarten. It's also great fun if you just want to live the life *you* choose.

Perspectives:

It all comes down to just one word

D uring a seminar a woman tried to sum up, more as a question than a statement of acceptance what I was asking the group to do. *"So you want me to just have faith?"* she said. *"Yes, I guess in a word that's what all of this comes down to"*. I replied. *"Faith"* is that non-tangible secret ingredient of life that is the catalyst that binds together all that we are and allows promise to gel into substance. Having faith is trusting in the incredible gift of creation that we are all a part of. Faith is knowing that we have the capacity to become so much more than our minds currently allow us to believe. Faith is the farmer, year after year who tills the soil in the spring. Plants the seed deep below the surface not knowing if the rains will come. Not knowing if the winds will blow. Not knowing if the birds will swoop down and steal it all away. Faith is simply planting the seed and holding fast to the belief that life itself will spring forth from it.

Here is what faith is not. Giving at every turn. Faith challenges our resolve with twists and turns along the path towards our destination. Faith weeds out the non believers and leaves them at the side of the road to make way for those whose resolve does not weaken from the strain of challenge. Faith is what the winner wakes up with every morning. Faith is what they take to bed at days end whether more has been placed in their basket or not. Faith is seeing past the obstacles, even when on occasion they may block out the sun itself. In the end those who hold fast to faith get to discover that it is the most exotic spice in the world and it is what makes victory taste as sweet as it does. At the end of the day it all comes down to one word. Its there. It's always been there. Over days and months and years we tend to get distracted and set it down. In a hurry most end up picking up the wrong one and carrying on through life. You will know when you find it. It's unmistakeable. I have been fortunate lately to listen to an entirely authentic voice coming of age. Our little girl turned four months old and has found hers. At first the shrieks that echoed throughout the house sent everyone running to see what was wrong with her. Nothing wrong we soon discovered. On the contrary, all seemed right. This tiny little person had discovered that she had a voice she could use at will and on purpose. A voice to trumpet to the world her joy and excitement looking up at the mobile suspended over her crib. A voice of glee, triumphant at the accomplishment of rolling over. A voice of urgency, connected to her stomach and sounding the alarms of hunger. Here is what her voice is most importantly. Oblivious to the concerns and opinions and encroachment of the world around us. Hers is the voice of belief. Hers is the voice of authenticity. The voice that simply, plainly, without boast or presumption of importance says. *"This is who I am"*.

If you have misplaced yours along the journey of life, take the time to find it. You will know when you do. It will sound crisp and clear. Loud and familiar. Stating exactly what it wants with complete and total disregard for what the world thinks. I hope you find it soon. My little girl needs more people to talk to.

Perspectives:

We all get just one lifetime

My entire goal working in this field of personal and professional growth is to hopefully find the right words to help others believe. Believe in themselves. Believe in the incredible gifts they were born with. Believe in the mix of raw materials and people and creativity and imagination that when properly stirred and coaxed can create legacies far beyond what most would think possible. I have an application on my I-phone called Cool Facts. Pretty self-explanatory. It contains a database of interesting facts. Waiting for an appointment I was flipping though it and came across this one. *"During their first year of operation the total gross sales for this company was $16,000"* That seemingly impossible statistic caused me to go online and see where the company was now. Here are a few interesting points. The company was founded in 1975. Their total revenue for 2008 topped $60 billion. Their main corporate campus, which serves as the head office today includes more than 750,000 m² (approx. 8 million square feet) and over 30,000 employees. That is only one facility. In total the company employees close to 90,000 people in 105 countries. Net income last year was over $17 billion. At last count the CEO, Bill Gates and his wife had donated over $24. billion to charity. Yes, Microsoft had very humble beginnings. What an amazing example of just what is possible in a lifetime. Here is a fact to consider. No one in the history of mankind has ever achieved what they did in more than one lifetime. We only get one. I don't want you to be impressed by this man. I would like you to be inspired. Inspired to believe that we all have our shot. We all have the capacity to create so much more than our mind is currently willing to allow us to believe. Know this then. We all get just one lifetime. Make yours spectacular. I'll be fascinated to see what Bill Gates does with the second half of his life. He's just 53.

Perspectives:

Find your other soul mate

The process of finding love is perhaps the least understood and blissfully so. This is an area where I pray science will not prod, poke and distil down the emotional and biological components and unseen forces of energy involved into a test-tube so that we can then take a pill or wear a patch to find true love. It is fascinating really when you consider that at this moment in time the world's population is said to be 6,794,420,529. That would be the haystack and your true love would in fact be the tiniest of needles. Yet we do. People by the millions do it every day. Love is the catalyst that perpetuates the species. While this may appear to be a romanticization of every relationship on every continent it is not. Finding love, true love many times requires more than simply a glance across a dance floor or a casual conversation at the fresh fruit market. Many times it involves an incredible leap of faith and courage and belief that aborts reason and challenges logic and public wisdom. We rented and watched a movie that made me think of this. It was called "Love Actually" with Hugh Grant. Bad movie actually but it provided fodder for this perspective. It pointed out the challenge and courage required to find true love and to hold onto it. It made me think of another movie that was good "actually". "The Bridges of Madison County" was a great movie and a true portrayal of the power of true love. It's the story of the country wife who meets the photographer and succumbs to reason over what she knows should have been to her destiny. In one scene towards the end of the movie, while sitting in the truck with her husband she sees him in the pouring rain and reaches out for the handle on the door. At the last minute she pulls back and they drive off. She never sees him again. The next time she hears of him it is of his death. All the could have, should have been's had washed away. The clock ticks for us all on what is possible. What a great metaphor for life and our goals and dreams. We are all deserving of a great destiny. We are all deserving of having our heart beat in our chest like a teenager in love while moving forward towards a life of passion. Settling for what is right and rationale and reasonable should be something for others and not for you. It will take courage and strength and conviction to not only find your life's passion but to have the courage to ask it out on a date. A date that could and should last a lifetime. A life of passion is possible for you if you reach out and turn the handle. Know this. It can be your other soul mate.

Perspectives:

When the final gust blows

There are fascinating metaphors of life that show up this time of the year. This being harvest time. Like the New Year this is a great time to reflect back on what we have done and look forward to what is possible. Oftentimes our hopes and dreams can be put on the back burner. *"I'll get to this later. I'll start that next week. I'll become that tomorrow"*. Sadly, the tomorrows have a way of piling up like drifts of snow in the winter. We have a favorite tree in the backyard. It's an Aspen and all summer long when the wind blows the leaves rustle and sound like a gentle rain. It towers over our back deck and hangs directly over the hot tub. Most mornings and most evenings I sit back there looking up into the leaves and listen to the wind play its tune of nature. As the temperatures began to drop the leaves quickly changed from a vibrant green to a dull yellow. There is no great fanfare of color like the maple. The leaves seemed to stay this pale color of yellow for the longest time. Then between yesterday and today when I wasn't watching a great many lost their fight with gravity and lie silent on the ground. While sitting outside today a gust of wind came up and stripped off almost every single last leaf. One big gust and then whoosh they were gone. I sat looking up wondering if this is how it feels at the end of life. Wondering if all those days and all those dreams and all of our potential comes undone and flutters back down to earth. At this moment in time we are all still in a very good place to take action and not allow our passion to die with us. Here is what all of this means I guess. We are here for a good while but for us all the seasons will change and the winds will blow. Stop and ask yourself this question right now. *"Will I be at peace with my time here when the final gust of wind blows"*?

I hope you enjoyed reading these few selections from Perspectives and that the urge is beginning to stir in you to do what is necessary to define your goals and to find your passion. There are two ways to go through life. They offer up two separate and distinct philosophies from which to live by. One says that you are to be responsible, work hard, trade life for money and do you best to find happiness with whatever time and money is left at the end of the day. The other is to design your life and make that your work. I know the process may be scary and I know it may feel impossible and I know you may say, sure, *"for them"* and not me but I implore you to choose passion. What I know with absolute certainty is that every one of us will die. Make the commitment now to be one of those who truly lives. Be that person who designs their own life and pulls it off.

Going through this process and committing to walking through the door of your life's potential was illustrated so well in the 1998 movie Sliding Doors with Gwyneth Paltrow. In the movie she played a character that was followed from one turning point in life through two different outcomes. In the movie she was let go from her job and asked to pack up her desk and leave. Carrying a box of personal processions to the street she stood crying in the rain waiting for a cab. As the cab pulled up she broke a heal on her shoe and while she was trying to fix it a man rushed in and took her ride. It took about 5 minutes to hail the next cab. Just before she arrived at her apartment her fiancé got the women out the door who he had been with in their bed just moments before. As a result she never caught him and her life continued on, leading to an unhappy life. Then the story rewound and a second scenario showed her hailing the cab, this time not breaking her heal and arriving home five minutes earlier to catch him in bed. As a result she kicked him out and her life went in an entirely different direction. This change brought her a completely different life of true love and happiness and fulfillment. I know this is just a movie but this is the crossroads you are potentially facing right now. Which fork in the road are you going to choose? Are you going to stay on the path you are on or are you going to commit to doing anything and everything to change direction and find your true love and passion? This is your life. This is your choice. This may be the most important decision you ever make in life. Do it. Go for it. Step forward towards all that you are deserving of and never look back.

We will now move on to discuss the exercise of defining your goals and discovering your passion. As was discussed in the introduction, I don't want this to merely entertain you but to forever change you. I want you to use this book as it was intended. This process will create the steps and stages of not only defining your goals and mission in life but it will also detail and provide structure to what is required to arrive at the destination of your choosing.

Exercise: Finding your passion

The reason I am driven to do this to help you to discover your passion on purpose is because almost 30 years ago I was one of the lucky ones. All the stars lined up at just the right moment and I tripped over it. I found my passion and took action to do something about it at the urging of a friend. If not for that day back in 1983 in my kitchen with a co-worker who asked the question, *"So what do you really want to do?"* I would not be where I am today. I don't want you to wait to see if by chance you may trip over it. I have dedicated my life to helping as many people possible find it on purpose. You can you know. By doing the work from the following exercise you will be able to discover your life's passion on purpose. This is not something possible for the few but for all who choose to invest the time in themselves. For once in your life be selfish and do this for you.

One final caveat before reviewing the exercise is to know that implementing a number of elements will be necessary in the upcoming chapters once you have discovered it to have it become your reality. Again, I suggest that you read through the exercise but wait to begin the work until after you have read the entire book and understand all the pieces to the puzzle. Viewing and accepting the entire process will make greater sense and offer much more structure than if you begin with just one element.

Exercise

Write the Movie of Your Life

This exercise is very different from the concept of goal setting or trying to define who you want to be, relative to where you are right now. We are all trained throughout life to set goals, however the problem that arises from major life goals is that when we attempt to identify what we don't currently have, the sub-conscious mind is all too quick to offer up all the reasons why we can't have it or why it may not work, now or for ever. In order to go inside and truly connect with what our passion is in life, we need to silence the voice and at least temporarily suspend the psychological obstacles.

The first element of the exercise is to begin with an understanding of how the brain works. The brain processes information in pictures, not in our day-to-day form of communication. If you are told to see an elephant, you don't see the letters E.L.E.P.H.A.N.T, you see a big floppy eared pachyderm. The same holds true for the process you are about to go through. Defining goals in picture form and then inserting yourself into the experience viewed through the motion picture of the mind's eye is what makes this possible and works to remove the obstacles. In essence what you will be doing is to define, write and create a motion picture with you as the lead actor. The second and most critical element of this is to not simply define what you want. This exercise will engage you from a creative standpoint to imagine and then visualize what you _already had_.

Let me explain. We are all capable of replaying the movie in our mind of past events. Everything from the vacations we attended, the birth of our children, buying our first home, graduation and so on. In effect what you will be instructed to do throughout this exercise is just that. To create a fictitious movie scene of what you are truly connected to emotionally from the perspective of having already experienced it. An example may be that you are living in the home of your dreams. You will design and define it down to the last detail and then insert yourself into the scene. Seeing yourself park in the driveway, walk up to the front door, enter inside, walking through the foyer, kitchen and den out through the patio doors where all your friends and family are waiting around the pool and fountain for the BBQ to begin will allow you to experience it mentally and to gage your emotional response to it. You are going to define the movie of your life. This is the first step to move you from where you are to where you deserve to be.

There is only one person who will star in the movie of your life. There can only ever be one person and that is you. The unfortunate reality is that the majority of people agree by default to star in the movie of their life that is not of their choosing. The world and those around us end up writing the script and directing our lives through opinion and influence. Know this. The writers are not unionized. You can fire them at this exact moment in time. You have the power to pick up the pen and begin to write your own script. You are without question going to be the one who is the lead actor. You should also be the one who writes the script and you have the power to do just that at this exact moment in time.

Developing the script and creating the plot for the lead character should be one of your great joys and most important tasks in life. We get faked out into believing in others as the leading men and women of the great movies rather than ourselves. We unfortunately allow society to write the script of how our lives will turn out.

The goal through this exercise is to clearly define the movie in our mind of where we are going and who we are on our way to becoming. Take control. Be the one who writes the script to *your* movie. You will know it when you find your life's purpose because it will make you feel *like this*. Like you did when your first child was born. Like you did the first day you realized you were in love. Like you did when your team hoisted you up and cheered your name because you won the day. Connecting to the goals in life that create emotion and passion is where you are going to go. Because they will make you *feel like this*. Those who find their passion feel it and as a result have the capacity to accomplish more than the world ever thought possible.

Where to Begin

The process of discovering your passion and vision in life will require you to go deep inside and connect to what it is that your heart truly beats for. The daily exercise to begin this is called the *"End of Life Perspective"*. Prior to beginning this exercise it is important for you to take the time to complete the Lifequest exercise below. Your response to the questions in this exercise will begin to uncover thoughts and experiences from your past that may have been covered up with years of negative input.

The following exercise is designed to help you strip away everything the world has ever told you to want and to find out what you want for yourself. Developing a passion or purpose in life changes everything. It alters the dynamic in life from pushing through our days to being pulled along towards our goals and our own personal vision of whom we desire to be. This discovery will provide the answers to "Why" am I doing this. "Why" am I here? "What" is my purpose?

Neil Donald Walsh, author of *"Conversations With God"* put this journey into a better perspective than I have ever heard it spoken. He said, *"Our mission in life is the mission we give ourselves"*

This may be the most important work you have ever done. Treat it as such. Set aside a time each day where you are free of distractions to answer the following questions and complete the exercise. It is of critical importance when answering the questions to continually ask the question, *"Do I want this for what society will think of me, or is this something that I truly want for myself?"* Identifying what you want solely for yourself in your own voice for your own reasons will uncover your authentic self and begin to create your vision.

Lifequest Exercise

Questionnaire

1) Name the most interesting people you have met?

2) What do you like to talk about more than anything? What conversation do you find most stimulating?

3) Describe your most rewarding experiences in life to date?

- In sport?

- In relationships?

- In business?

- Helping others?

- In personal achievement?

4) What was your most exciting purchase?

5) What is your favorite form of entertainment?

6) What were your dreams as a child?

7) What were your most enjoyable activities as a child?

8) What have your dreams been as an adult?

9) What were your most enjoyable activities as an adult?

10) What unique gifts do you have? What activities come easily to you?

11) What do you clearly understand that the average person does not?

12) Who would you like to spend a day with if you could?

13) What would you talk about?

14) What skills and philosophy would you hope to share with others?

15) If your really knew me, you would know that?

16) What accomplishments of others do you admire?

17) What would an unlimited supply of money allow you to do?

18) What would more time allow you do?

19) What would you like to do to help others?

20) What skills would you like to have?

- 1
- 2
- 3

21) If this were your last day on earth, how would you spend your time excluding involvement with loved ones?

Discovering your vision

You are now ready to begin the work to define what you want your life to represent. The best place to begin your quest is from, as this exercise is titled *"An End of Life Perspective"*. The process of unlocking the answer to our life's purpose is best served by approaching it from a vantage point free of obstacles. As such, each day you will work to go inside from the perspective of looking back over your life from your last day on earth. This of course will be a fictitious exercise.

Spending the time alone everyday in quiet meditation, reflecting on, what for you was a perfect life, will allow you to begin to discover the answers that elude so many people today. This exercise will take time. Allow it to happen. This is perhaps the most important task that you will accomplish in moving forward in designing an authentic life. I cannot stress enough how important it is for you to do the work to uncover your own vision. Finding your passion will provide the fuel to make everything possible in the weeks and months and years to come. This movie will become your own.

Daily Exercise

Here is the structure of the exercise. Each day you are to find a place free of distraction for a period of just 10 minutes. 10 minutes is a good amount of time to allow for the creative process to begin taking hold. Once you are in your place you are to visualize this. You are 96 years old sitting comfortably in a chair with the understanding that this is your last day on earth. You are dying today. You are at total peace with this because you have had the perfect life. You had it all. From this day until your end of life you had and became and went and enjoyed all that really mattered and your heart was connected to.

Each day you are to take one of the questions detailed below into the exercise with you. Take in only one question each day and follow through the list in sequence each day. Before you begin the exercise each day, take a few moments to clear your mind of thought and distractions. Again, the perspective you are approaching this from is that it is your last day on earth and you are looking back over your life. What you are looking back over was a perfect life with everything that made it complete and fulfilled, exciting and rewarding for you.

Take a notepad in with you and at the end of the 10-minute session write down what you thought about, imagined and most importantly make note of how you felt. Here is the list of questions from which you will use one each day. Once you gone through all of the questions start over at the beginning and keep going until you have clear and concise answer to each and every one of them.

- What did I love?

- What did I do?

- What did I have?

- Where did I go?

- Who did I become?

- What did I accomplish?

- Who were the important people in my life?

- What example did I set for my children?

- What was my legacy?

This exercise and the answers to the questions above will begin to form the foundation of discovering your true passion and purpose in life. This is the first step in enabling you to empower yourself to one day soon lead the life you always wondered was possible. Complete this exercise everyday until you have a clear set of answers to all of the questions above. It is of great importance to remind yourself to enjoy this journey. Learning to live on purpose is a fascinating experience and this journey as much as your arrival at the destination should be experienced and not missed.

Creating the Scene From The Movie of Your Life

The foundation of this process is of course is to identify the vision of how you want your life to turn out. Once the *End of Life Perspective* exercise has been completed and you have a clear answer to all of the questions what you are then to do in the space provided below is to write a scene or snapshot from the movie of your life incorporating much of what you have identified as the keys to the vision of your life. This brief screenplay will serve as the daily guiding motivation of your activity moving forward. Once written, you will then replay it everyday and use it to visualize the life you have chosen. An example of a scene would be that *"you are here, with these people, experiencing this and feeling the overwhelming emotion that accompanies it"*. This is the key that will provide the fuel to do what is necessary to become who you are deserving of. Again, once the End of Life Perspective exercise is complete and you have a clear and concise answer to every question you are then ready to write a scene from the movie of your life that incorporates much of what you have identified in the exercise.

_____

_____

_____

_____

_____

_____

_____

_____

_____

_____

_____

_____

_____

_____

_____

_____

_____

_____

_____

_____

_____

_____

_____

_____

_____

_____

Gratitude is an important element in the soup of success. Having gratitude for what we have at this exact moment in time opens the door for more. Focusing on what you have will enlighten the process of what is possible to come in the future. Having come from a difficult childhood, I wrote these words a great many years ago and they have always served me. They are;

I am grateful for where I came from

I am grateful for where I am

I am grateful for where I am going

I understand that what you are considering doing and what you believe is possible may appear far off in the distance. The great strides our species has made over the centuries have not come about by adhering to the status quo. It will take determination and courage to walk your own path however there is nothing more authentic than being comfortable in your own skin. There was an advertising piece written for Apple computers that embodied the essence of the company back in the late 90's. These words are your words. These are the words that move those unique individuals forward and separate those who merely trade life for money from those who design a life. Read these words and make them your own.

"Here's to the crazy ones. The misfits. The rebels. The trouble-makers. The round pegs in the square holes. The ones who see things differently. They're not fond of rules, and they have no respect for the status-quo. You can quote them, disagree with them, glorify, or vilify them. But the only thing you can't do is ignore them. Because they change things. They push the human race forward. And while some may see them as the crazy ones, we see genius. Because the people who are crazy enough to think they can change the world, are the ones who do". —Apple

Once you discover your true goals and link your purpose to your passion you will be in the absolute minority. Here is what is also essential to know and accept in order to see this through to its end. There are a number of other aspects of our being that must be brought into concert in order for your passion to see the light of day. As Lau Tsu said, *"The journey of a thousand miles begins with the first step"*. This is the first step. Just as it is not possible to arrive at our destination by taking just one step, there are other steps that are essential to transition this from an inspired thought to and inspired life. Stay with me. Over years of creating and implementing coaching programs for thousands of individuals, what I have learned is that in order to get there, (achieve your goal) you must first understand how you got here. Now we begin at the beginning; but first the story of the writer. This is my story.

The Writer-My Story

I n those days, I always got off the bus alone. Being the youngest of four by a few years meant that my two older brothers and sister had long since changed bus routes and escaped into high school. I was 11 at the time. Our house was a small wood-framed bungalow in the country, stuck in the middle of a square plot of land, surrounded by cornfields and vineyards. A few of the neighbors' homes boasted of the success of the wine industry. In the laneways of some homes, shiny new cars were parked along manicured lawns. If you drove down our road, you couldn't help but notice the stark contrast from one property to the next.

As the bus pulled away, I looked back over my shoulder to see kids from both sides of the tracks riding together. It was a rolling microcosm of the social structure of this rural community. I walked up the driveway and up the steps to the front door. It was locked. We never locked our house. Living in the country and in a house like ours didn't exactly make you a mark for the criminal element. Peering through one of the small diamond-shaped windows in the faded front door, I was able to make out the form of someone sprawled on the living-room floor - my mother. She lay face down, not moving. Her arms and legs were splayed like those of a rag doll that had been tossed aside. A pool of dark liquid spilled out on the floor from around her head.

After pounding on the door and calling for help, the fear inside sent me racing for the neighbors'. Within minutes I was back with a neighbor who was a nurse. She broke one of the panes of glass, opened the front door and administered first aid. My worst fears weren't realized that day. She hadn't killed herself. This wasn't another thwarted suicide attempt.

My mother had merely gotten drunk and fallen, hitting the bridge of her nose on the coffee table, which had caused the extensive bleeding. She'd staggered around the house, leaving a trail of blood everywhere before passing out on the floor. While the neighbor was bringing her to, I called my father at work, frantic and wanting someone to make this all to go away. When I blurted into the phone what had happened, he said, *"Look, I'm at work and can't take time off. There's nothing I can do. She'll be fine. I'll be home later."* And he hung up.

This is an excerpt from life growing up in a family with challenges. When it's happening to you in the moment, it all seems to move in slow motion. The thought of one day being free of the violent fights, constant threats of suicide, loneliness and gripping fear seemed so far off in the distance. Looking back, I can see that it was that flicker of light of what could be that pushed me to get past those days and vow to never accept that that was where I belonged. I know now that life's most difficult challenges are what push us to reach inside for the resolve not just to survive but also to make something from the mess. When you're fortunate and make it out, people say you're resilient. I think it just gives you a better way to measure life: The first goal is to fight your way to normal, and once you get there, the challenge of reaching for something extraordinary isn't so daunting. In more ways than you can know I'm grateful for those days as a child.

Getting from where I was to where I am today was the easiest and most difficult thing I've ever done. The most difficult because I had to discover on my own the essence of what holds people back and then how to overcome the self-limiting behavior that devours dreams; the easiest because once I did begin to overcome it, discovering my passion and working toward my goal has been the most liberating and uplifting experience of my life – it's simply what I had to do.

After bankruptcy knocked our family down when I was very young, my father spent more and more time at work and we continued to struggle financially. My mother, who, like most, was a stay-at-home mom, was left alone. She suffered from a number of medical problems and was hospitalized more times than I can count. The bright lights and antiseptic smell of hospitals has left an imprint in my memory that will likely never go away. Like too many women of the day, she was prescribed "mother's little helper." Before long, the combination of pills, illness and loneliness created a powerful addiction.

Many people who live with alcoholic or drug-addicted family members will tell you the same thing. When they're sober or straight, they can be the most wonderful people in the world. When they're drunk or high, they can be among the most vile and hurtful. And you never give up hoping. You never really let go of the dream that they'll beat it and choose you over the bottle. I ended running away and lived on the streets when I was 14 because of it all; seeing my mother's life spiral out of control and the violent atmosphere it created was too much to bear.

It's fascinating thinking back now that that was where I lived given that I won't let my kids go to the end of the driveway. Shortly after that she moved away to be with her addiction. I can't judge her, because I don't really know what she went through. Her illness, loneliness and addiction had robbed her of a life she deserved to live. One of her favorite sayings that I have kept with me and cherished was *"Don't judge another until you've walked a mile in their moccasins,"* and I hadn't walked in hers. Occasionally, I would hear that she had moved here or there, but I didn't see her for the next 10 years. She was never able to beat the addiction and passed away in her early sixties.

A difficult childhood can have a powerful impact on your life and your belief system. Society seems to predetermine the pecking order of our lives depending on our social status. It was just understood that kids like us would take our place and fall in line. We were looked upon as the kids who would go on to work in manual labor or construction or, maybe if we worked hard, some kind of trade. The irony is that we bought into it even though we were going through our rebellious years. Few people who come from that *"side of the tracks"* question the logic of their place in this world. We accepted that that was where we would end up and where we belonged. The thought of becoming a doctor or a lawyer or a scientist or a writer never entered our minds. Those jobs were for the kids who came from great homes and had the necessary support, both personal and financial.

Over the years, I went from job to job. Gradually, the jobs got better and I was able to break the mold financially. By all accounts, I was doing very well. I had a wife and son, owned my own home with two cars, was able to take vacations and had food on the table. The voices of society spoke up over the din of my life, telling me I had far more than I deserved and should be very grateful. It was troubling to hear those voices and believe they were right. It was more unsettling to have come as far as I had and feel miserable. Looking back I now know that I was one of the fortunate ones who realized that something was missing. The real turning point in my life was on the day I left high school at age 16, as I was walking out the door my guidance councilor said something that stayed with me. He said, *"Randy I want you to always know something. That where you are now has nothing to do with where you can go"*. That statement allowed me to begin to challenge the status quo and push back against the voices of society. It changed my life.

One sunny Friday afternoon in early December 1983 I was sitting in my kitchen with Tom, a co-worker at a large sales firm I'd just left. It had been a great job with a company car and an expense account, but I'd felt trapped. I didn't want *"account manager"* to be written on my tombstone the way it was embossed on the upper right-hand corner of my business cards. I knew there had to be more.

"So, what do you want to do with your life?" Tom asked. I told him something I hardly told anyone. I said, , *"You know Tom, since I was a little kid I thought it would be amazing to be the guy on the radio."* That was my passion. Deep down, I knew it was something I'd wanted since I was a little kid, but I hadn't pursued it because I listened to all the reasons that I would probably fail. I'd heard them all: The competition is too great; thousands of students are coming out of colleges every year; you'll never make a

living at it; you're too old. I'd heard the reasons so many times over the years that they felt like they were my own.

Tom was a great guy and a bit of a dreamer himself. *"So, why don't you call a radio station and see what you have to do or where to go to school?"* he said. After making several calls to the major-market stations to the south in Toronto and being given the standard *"Send in your tape and resume,"* I decided to call the local station. After a few minutes on the phone with the program director, I hung up and Tom asked, *"Well, what'd he say?"* *"You're not going to believe this"* I said. *"He wants to see me on Monday"*.

That was it. That's how it all started. I was 28 years old. After the interview, I was hired part time to work the board and within a week to do fill-in work on-air. For the next year and three months, I worked as the weekend overnight announcer for 12 hours a week at $4.25 an hour. Keep in mind that I had a young family to provide for and that $42 a week left me just a touch short. During that time, I did anything and everything I could to make ends meet. I worked at a grocery store stocking shelves from midnight till 8 in the morning. I sold cars, cleaned swimming pools and eventually started my own swimming-pool company out of my garage.

Finally I was hired full time when a shift came open for the evening show. It paid $9,000 a year. This was a quarter of what I was making in the sales job I'd had before starting in radio, but I was never happier in my life. There was never a day that I wasn't excited to get to work. This was my passion. There's no feeling like the feeling of living your passion. You laugh more, require less sleep, handle stress better and look forward to getting up every morning, excited to see what the day will bring.

The move up and down the dial took me to Ottawa, then back to Toronto. During my last three years in radio, I was the drive-home talk-show host at the largest station in Canada. The dream of having a daytime shift and making enough to support my family had been a reality for 20 years. If you ever worry about the money, don't. When you do something that's your passion, you will excel at it because to you it will never be work and you will in turn be rewarded. Never worry about the money. If you're doing what you love, your work will be recognized and the money will be there.

The journey from where I was to where I am today has been extraordinary. Nine years ago I shut off the microphone for the last time and entered this field of personal and professional development. While I had no education or training in this field I had studied the science of human behavior for over 30 years. When I left broadcasting I did not have one client. What I did have was a passion bigger than all the outdoors to do this. To work with others and do anything and everything I could to make them own that question that changed everything for me. *"What if where you are now has nothing to do with where you can go"?* My passion has been rewarded in ways I could never have imagined. My client list now reads like the who's who of corporate finance. The coaching programs I created, EPIC, The Winner Within and Breakthrough Coach have now received national accreditation from some of the largest financial services companies in the world. Now with the release of this book I am so far beyond where I imagined all those years ago that words just can't do this justice

I I'm so grateful for being able to live my dreams that I sometimes have a hard time grasping the fact that it happened to me. There's not a day that goes by when I don't think about how fortunate I am and how much my life has changed. All those voices that I listened to for all those years that said I would fail were wrong. They're wrong for you, too. Just like the group you are about to join, I'm one of those fortunate ones who can say without hesitation, *"I'm living the life I was meant to live"*.

2

How did I get here?

"What lies behind us and what lies before us are small matters compared to what lies within us." – Emerson

I n the book The Alchemist by Paulo Calheo the character Santiago talked often of finding his personal legend. This is the journey you are about to embark upon. We will begin from that place long ago before your belief system was impacted by the world around you. You are embarking on finding your own personal legend or vision of what life should be for you. That is a life lived on purpose with passion and drive. To feel every day that you are alive with a reason. It is fascinating to think that as you are reading these first few chapters that a thought could be forming and an emotion long buried is beginning to stir and take shape that will allow you to live the life you are so deserving of.

The process of discovering your passion and inserting it into your life in such a way that you too will live the life you are deserving of will require a number of steps. The next is to understand how you got here. This entire process of discovering our life's vision is based upon and centered on your personal belief system. Before we start to delve into what subverted the perfect belief system you were born with it is critical to know what you posses. You must first come to terms with and appreciate what you are given at birth. The truth is that it is more than you can possibly know.

"So what makes you think everyone can achieve his or her dreams"? I've heard this question countless times. The reason I'm so certain that you will be able to achieve your dreams is because I know and understand that you have now and have always had everything you ever needed to become anything you could ever want. I have also had the great privilege to see this happen for countless others over my time in this field.

To truly appreciate the potential we have within us, I believe, it's critical to recognize that the playing field we're given is much more even than you've been led to believe. It's the miracle of life that provides an equal start for us all. The obstacles we encounter, the doubts we develop and the challenges we face all result from input from the people and experiences that surround us after birth.

How our lives begin and the miracle we are given is truly remarkable. What happens to most of us is that we squander that gift when we give up the ability to choose. Remember, it's about choice. We can choose to believe the word *can't* does or does not exist. The journey to come to terms with this, while challenging, is the same for us all. We can choose to "settle" and become what is expected of us or choose to follow our dreams.

"We are all born naked and screaming, and if you're lucky that sort of thing won't stop there." -- Unknown

What we're going to go through in the coming pages may appear to be an anatomy lesson, but I believe it's important to spend the time to come to terms with all we are given. It will give you a sense of what you're capable of by coming to terms with how astounding your creation really is. By grasping just how complex we are, we can then begin to understand that following our dreams isn't as difficult as we once thought. When I first began studying human anatomy and physiology it had a profound impact on my life. I had never felt so humble. Life's current challenges seem positively inconsequential when compared with what we are all capable of at birth. I hope this information has the same impact on you.

Let's start with your creation. From a single cell, the fertilized egg grows to become a complex human being consisting of trillions of cells, each one capable of billions of functions. The details of this process could fill a library, and yet we all take our beginning for granted. Consider that the average person lives for about 30,000 days, give or take a few, and yet the time it takes to create human life is just 280 days.

During that time, a single sperm implants itself in an egg, and development continues as the pre-embryo travels through the uterine tube, floating free in the cavity of the uterus, finally implanting in the uterine wall. Within 36 hours, cell division has begun, and by the fourth or fifth day after fertilization, the pre-embryo consists of only about 100 cells. By five weeks, the embryo begins to resemble a tadpole, and the formation of a thyroid gland, an esophagus, a trachea, lungs, a stomach, a liver, a pancreas, a gallbladder, intestines and a heart has begun.

Over the next 35 weeks, the metamorphosis from that tadpole into a fully functioning human being is something that mankind will never truly grasp. I recall my wife and I reading through a book on fetal development when she was pregnant with our daughter. At one stage, I believe about 12 weeks into the pregnancy, we read that the heart had now formed into the four chambers and was beginning to pump blood throughout the body by way of the circulatory system. It also said that at that time, the heart was about the size of a poppy seed. Incredible to believe that by 40 weeks, the baby was ready to be born.

We all come into the world as complete human beings, capable of transforming oxygen and food into energy, controlling nerve endings and muscle groups through movement, and forming thought patterns in reaction to our surroundings. What was the most amazing aspect of my research was what our bodies are capable of doing from the moment we're born. Keep in mind that these functions are all in working order after just 280 days since conception -- less than the average hockey season. The intelligence inherent in our bodies is so vast that it's positively staggering. If you ever need to be humbled by your own creation, pick up this book and leaf through the following pages. It will put anything we accomplish into perspective and make us realize what's truly amazing and how equal we all are at birth.

The human heart beats about 100,000 times every 24 hours. Consider the fact that the heart pumps six quarts of blood throughout your body every day. That's the equivalent of 6,300 gallons of blood being pumped per day. That's almost 115 million gallons in just 50 years. The six quarts of blood are made up of more than 24 trillion cells that make three to five thousand trips throughout the body every day. Seven million new blood cells are produced every second. This pumping system has the capability of working nonstop for decades without skipping a beat, and this is only the circulatory system.

Consider the heat your body must generate in accomplishing these functions while maintaining a constant temperature of 98.6 degrees. The biggest organ of the body, the skin, is made up of over 4 million pores that are constantly acting as the cooling system for this machine. The digestive and metabolic systems have the remarkable ability to transform the food we eat into healthy bone, blood and cell structure. Perfect balance is always maintained, and if it were off by only a small fraction, the balance would be destroyed.

The lungs succeed in supplying the blood with the oxygen it needs. A complex skeletal system furnishes a supporting framework to allow the body to stand upright and walk. The skeletal system works in harmony with an amazing muscular system that allows for locomotion.

The five senses alone can stun the intellect. The list of activities your body performs on a regular basis could fill a library. And at the helm of this pinnacle of perfection is the brain, overseeing all these miraculous activities, making sure everything is working with a precision that would make the work of a master watchmaker look clumsy. The brain consists of more than 100 billion cells or neurons that are the most highly developed of any known.

A single cell can't be seen without a microscope, yet the wisdom within just one cell is said to contain all the accumulated knowledge of the human race to date. Even the smallest cell in your body is about 1 billion times the size of its smallest component. The cell is the site of more chemical reactions than occur in a day in all the chemical factories in the world combined. There are thousands of components in a cell: chromosomes, genes, DNA, organelles, mitochondria, enzymes, hormones, amino acids, chemicals and compounds too numerous to mention. All the thousands of functions can be categorized, but the force behind the functions is beyond our comprehension.

To think that there are more than 75 trillion of these astounding cells working with pinpoint perfection for 70, 80, 90 years or more.

If you took all the DNA from all the genes in all your 75 trillion cells, it would fit into a box the size of an ice cube. Yet if all this DNA were unwound and joined back together, the string would stretch from the Earth to the sun and back again more than 400 times.

To help you understand the size of the numbers we're talking about and the cooperation necessary to coordinate them, try this: Imagine all 7 billion of the Earth's inhabitants working in unison.   Now imagine 18,000 Earths, each with 7 billion inhabitants and every last one working in unison. All have the same political beliefs, and all are working for the exact same goal. That's precisely what the trillions of cells in your body do every day for decades.

As one last illustration of how incredible the human body is, imagine yourself writing an extremely important letter to a friend while simultaneously watching your favorite TV program and listening to a positive-mental-attitude tape.   How well would you perform these functions? Probably not very well.

Your body is performing quadrillions of processes simultaneously 24 hours a day. Not millions or billions or even trillions but quadrillions. And not haphazardly but with pinpoint perfection, carrying on all the metabolic and life sustaining processes of your existence.

When we're born, we're all in possession of the same incredible systems that make up the human body. When you consider what we've been through and have accomplished during the 280 days it took to create us, the rest of our lives is truly a gift. What determines who we are and what we become is a direct result of what we do with this gift.

"Men are equal: it is not birth but virtue that makes the difference" -- *Voltaire*

The question must then be, *"If we are all born equal, why do we experience such different outcomes in our lives?"* The answer is conditioning through the experiences of day-to-day life. Before we are able to communicate, ignorance of the word *can't* leads us to accept *can* as our driving force. Before we are able to communicate, we're like an ant that's trying to carry a piece of wood or an insect back to its hill. It will go around, over and through anything to complete the job or die trying. It has no concept of not completing the task.

I remember years ago watching my oldest son, Justin, when he was a few months old sitting in his walker. Someone had given him this big, bright red plastic apple that was weighted funny and rolled from side to side. When you pushed it back and forth, it made music, and he was quite taken with it. Like the ant that knows only of getting the insect back to his hill, his sole mission was to get that apple into his mouth. At birth all babies are born without motor skills or muscle control. The fascinating thing to watch was his determination and focus on the task at hand. He just wouldn't give up.

The simple action of trying to close his fingers around the stem at the top was something he had to learn from the beginning. One finger would wrap around the stem, and then he'd try to squeeze it by getting his thumb involved but in doing so would let go with the first finger. This went on and on and on.

When he'd finally managed to master gripping more than one finger around the stem, he'd lift it to put it in his mouth and it would slip out and fall onto the floor or the tray of the walker. If it landed on the tray, he'd try all over again. If it hit the floor, he'd look at me, begin waving his pudgy little legs from between the straps of the stroller and make an "uh, uh, uh" noise until I got the message and put it back on his tray for him.

He tried as many ways as he could think of to get it to his mouth; one hand, two hands, between his forearms. Nothing worked. At one point he figured out that it might be easier if he tried to bring his mouth down halfway. There he was, fingers twisted and contorted around the stem of the apple, his head bent toward it, mouth open and drool running down his chin. The apple would get halfway to its destination and he'd lose his grip, and the process would start all over.

I watched him try this for hours and days and weeks until he was finally able to do it. In total he likely tried well over 1,000 times to pick up the apple. The look of sheer joy on his face when he did was priceless. I will never forget that moment. It was a moment that began my serious quest into the study of human behavior. In that moment it dawned on me that the only reason he didn't stop trying was because no one told him he couldn't. I joke with audiences all the time that *"he's 34 years old now, and you should see him hold an apple. We are very proud of him"*.

To truly understand and appreciate the enormity of what it was that my son did, you first have to understand a bit about human anatomy and physiology. If this is beginning to sound like just another proud parent crowing over the accomplishments of his son, rest assured that I understand that this is nothing unique to him. We've all performed this incredible feat at some point and gone unrecognized for it. What he was able to accomplish took hundreds and perhaps thousands of attempts. To get that apple to his mouth, like all children, he had to train himself to control millions of nerve endings, thousands of muscle groups, tendons and ligaments. When we're born, we don't have the control over motor skills. It must be learned through constant trial and error. This is the kind of persistence that we rarely see in the adult world.

All of us have witnessed similar tests of human spirit and determination, probably without giving it any thought. Society rarely takes notice of the unbelievable accomplishments of learning to roll over, walk, talk or chew our food. All these tasks take a much greater level of determination than we demonstrate later in life, yet they go unnoticed and are taken for granted. They should in fact serve as examples throughout our lives.

Quitting or giving up becomes a part of our life philosophy not through nature but rather nurture. It's not something inherent in our genetic makeup. And it becomes increasingly entrenched in us over many years. But while the doubts created over many years of life experience, it's something that can be overcome and in effect *"unlearned."* Understanding the power of *can't* and acknowledging that it exists is the first step to returning to a life where anything is possible.

The next chapter will give you a firm understanding of how the experiences of the world that surround us has the capacity to develop self-limiting behavior. To use a war analogy, in the coming pages you will be instructed in how to identify the enemy.

What it looks like, what it sounds like and where it's most likely to be lurking in your life. Once identified, you will then be able to set out a plan to overcome it.

One final point: Don't delude yourself into believing that simply because you understand this theory, doors will automatically open and your dreams will fall at your feet. Know that whatever you're going to achieve is going to be attained through hard work, perseverance and a conscious commitment. Understanding the theory will only provide the keys to the kingdom. What you do with them will take determination and focus and drive. Next the story of the kid who loved sports. Then, on to the creation of the voice that is in truth the greatest nemesis to success.

The Boy who Loved Baseball

T he visible traces of the winter of 1982 began to disappear in the rearview mirror as the car plodded along interstate 25 en route to Florida. Dan sat in the backseat with his two younger sisters studying a book on baseball. Nothing unusual about that for a 12 year old boy except for the fact that the book he was studying consisted of over 300 pages of nothing but the statistics of every player in the major leagues. As a boy gifted in mathematics the numbers on the pages became much more than that. They represented the crack of the bat. An umpire shouting, "Yer ouuuuuuuuuuuuuuuut" and a short stop digging a ball out of the dirt in one motion, firing it to first base to gun the runner out. His love of sport remained a constant throughout life.

Growing up in an upper middle class family he was raised to follow the path to success that society cries for often. *"A good education. A good job. A good living. To be a good husband and father and a fine example in the community".* And so it was. His years growing up were typical for the time. Summers away at camp and cheering on baseball. Winters were spent following hockey.

Recognizing his gift early on for mathematics it seemed natural that this would somehow figure into his education and career. After graduating from high school with honors he enrolled to study actuarial science at Western University. Throughout his 4 years in university his mathematical gifts and work ethic character instilled by his parents paid off and he graduated with honors in 1986. Soon after, Dan landed a job with a large insurance company and began his career.

Along with meeting his future wife, Dan was also able to do something else at university. He was able to feed his love of sports. During the first semester he walked down to the school newspaper to sign up to volunteer as a sports writer. Rounding the corner he saw a line up of fellow students snaking down the hallway. His impatience got the better of him and he turned to walk away. As he was about to leave, a sign caught his eye that read, "Campus Radio". No one was standing in line so Dan walked in and signed up to volunteer to do some sports broadcasting. He wasn't very good but he did enjoy the few shifts he was given.

It was two years into his tenure with the insurance company when he shocked his family and fiancée by announcing that he was leaving his career to try his hand at broadcasting. To say the least they were all very nervous. So much time and effort and money had been invested in getting him to where he was and it made no sense to throw this all away.

"I'm going to give this two years" he promised. *"If I can't make a go of it by that time I'll go back to the insurance business".*

His first job in the radio was more than an hour away at a little station to the north. Minimum wage was the best he could expect for the shifts no one else wanted. Dan continued making the trip up and down the highway for the better part of a year and a half. Finally one day a larger radio station offered him the chance to try out for a weekend position.

When his weekend was over he was crushed when told that he was not good enough and was sent back. It would have been easy to quit but Dan kept going. Honing his skills and getting a bit better each day. Months passed and the same station that had sent him packing gave him another chance. This time he was ready. A great many days have been spent behind the microphone since that first day. Dan heard all the excuses over the years of why the odds were stacked against him. Early in 2010 the telephone rang at his parents home in Toronto. It was a family friend calling to congratulate them on the news that Dan had just been picked by Sports Illustrated as the play-by-play announcer of the decade. Early in 2011 he was picked for the top job in sports broadcasting as the play-by-play announcer of Sunday Night Baseball. A few months ago he was signed to he longest contract ever offered by ESPN. If you follow sports you no doubt have listened to or watched Dan Shulman on ESPN calling games for major league baseball, the NBA and college basketball. I now his story well. He's the brother of the woman I married. It all came to be from that one seemingly insignificant moment. That moment in the hallway of a university when for a young lover of sports, opportunity knocked. You are reading this story because he answered. An answer that every day has had him living the life he deserved.

3

Whose voice is it anyway?

I f we all have a passion in life or a personal journey, the obvious question is why so few of us actually act on it. As was pointed out in the previous chapter, the primary reason is the intake of negative information that begins to turn belief into doubt. For most of us, our passion has been stripped away and we've been made to feel incapable. The passion that may have once burned bright may now be pushed far beneath the surface. For many it may have been pushed so far back that it's difficult to recall exactly what that passion was.

The proof of our lost passion can be found in the dreams of a child. When we were children, our ability to dream was bigger than life. In fact, we were encouraged to live out our fantasies and passions through play, role-modeling and made-up games. Little girls dress up like adults and pose as singers or dancers or movie stars. Little boys feign being policemen, firefighters, lion tamers or superheroes. As children, we naturally gravitate toward the things we have a passion for. No one tells us it's wrong to dream. No one is likely to point out that the pay may be low for lion tamers or that the job opportunities are drying up for superheroes. Because of this, we end up totally immersed into our passion of the moment. We make great superheroes and ballerinas because no one tells us we can't. That comes much later, when we're faced with the onset of adulthood. That's when we're consistently reminded to grow up and be responsible. There's nothing rewarding about being called childlike in an adult world.

So if we are born perfect and we are, then what happens that changes all of that? That question has become my life's work. The answer can be found in the unique attributes of what it means to be human. Consider this. One of the most difficult things to come to terms with is that thing we can't see, yet has such an enormous impact on the outcome of our lives. That is our belief system. What we believe we can achieve, what we doubt gets left out. Again, when we are born our belief system is absolutely perfect and allows us the kind of persistence that provides for anything. As we age and we are bombarded with negative information it dissipates. This belief system is also what makes our species so unique.

You can't ask a tree to grow to only half its size. It's not possible. A tree will grow to the maximum of its potential because of the genetic code. It knows no other way. Humans are the only species that don't innately strive to reach its full potential. The reason is that we've been given the ability to choose. People are the only species who limit their capacity by choice. The reason some of us limit our capacity more than others is that we allow the influence of society and the intake of information through hundreds of thousands of interactions to have a greater effect on our belief systems. The more we bow to societal influences, the more flawed our philosophy of life becomes. We're all born with a perfect philosophy. It's the experiences we have throughout life that begin to chip away at that perfect belief system that originally allowed for a persistence and determination that we rarely see in the adult world.

"Only those who dare to go too far can possibly find out

how far they can go." -T.S. Eliot

If you have struggled to identify your passions and achieve your dreams, you're not alone. The majority of us has felt a block or is at a standstill, unable to take the steps to be true to our innermost desires and callings.

We often take note of those around us who have lived their passions and achieved remarkable success and assume that they excelled because of some extraordinary gifts. In reality, their "gift" was being able to grasp one of the most simplistic philosophies of life. They discovered that everything they needed for success was right there inside of them. In truth, it's inside all of us.

What stops us from believing in our dreams is that we've bought into the teachings of society. We accept the notion that advantages such as a privileged upbringing, better schools, nicer clothes, the right genes and a lucky break are the reasons that some succeed. Sadly, for most, that's the perception, but it certainly isn't the reality. At the moment that we're born, there are no winners and no losers. In the previous chapter, it was shown that at birth we all begin with the same incredible abilities. These gifts are what create a level playing field for us all.

If we all begin on equal footing, how does life become so unbalanced? The answer can be found in the Latin term *Tabula rasa,* which means, "blank slate." It's the concept that individual human beings are born "blank," with no built-in mental content, and that their identities are defined entirely by events that occur after birth. Through personal experience and interviews with hundreds of others who have overcome extraordinary odds, it became clear to me that the imbalance of success from one person to the next is due to society's influence over personal choice. This influence is something I refer to as negative conditioning

When I use the term *negative conditioning,* I would like to be clear on my definition of it. It's important to distinguish between the common understanding of *negative,* which is something that's bad for us, and the *negative* I refer to as a force to control choice. This negative is the pressure that society, throughout life, puts on us to buy into someone else's theory or logic. When we allow our dreams to be affected by the opinions of society, we allow doubt to begin to chip away at their veneer. Before long, the sheen disappears from our dreams and we succumb to the mere thought of the possibility of failure. In truth, no one could ever understand your passion. Passion is not about logic; it's about self-actualization.

Society's interference with your ability to choose can be demonstrated in all areas of interest and endeavor and throughout all stages of life. It has permeated our lives so deeply and so effectively that its acceptance has become almost universal.

It's fascinating when we finally come to the realization that the path our lives have taken, the skills we've acquired, the jobs we hold, the foods we enjoy and our political views have been determined almost entirely by the influence of those around us. First understanding and then learning to control negative conditioning will provide the key to unlock the untold potential inside of you.

> *"Man becomes a slave to his constantly repeated acts. What he at first chooses, at last compels." -- Orison Swett Marden*

The power of negative conditioning over our ability to choose is not achieved after just a few incidents. The reason it is able to imprint its will so effectively on our psyche is that it begins from the moment we are able to communicate and exerts its power thousands of times throughout our lives. It's the cumulative effect that's responsible for the creation of our self-limiting behavior.

This theory of repetitive-action conditioning was proven in an experiment more than 100 years ago. In the early 1900s, Russian scientist Ivan Pavlov became famous for his experiment on the effects of behavior conditioning on dogs. His initial experiment was on digestion and its relation to salivation. Quite by accident, he stumbled on the fact that dogs could be conditioned to salivate simply by ringing a bell. The process is called "neutral stimulus," defined as "the use of a stimulus not normally known to produce a response." During the experiment, a bell was rung just prior to the dogs' being fed. The process was repeated hundreds of times until it eventually caused the dogs to salivate in anticipation of the food without the food's actually being present.

Obviously, if the bell had been rung only a few times before a dog was fed, the experiment would have failed. The reason the dog salivated every time the bell sounded is that the action was repeated so often that it created a conditioned behavioral response. For people, negative conditioning creates a response similar to that of "Pavlov's dog." The result is that after many years of being conditioned by the influence of society, we begin to exhibit self-limiting behavior.

What many people may not know about Pavlov's experiment is that he was also able to show that the behavior could be unlearned. He discovered that if the bell was rung over and over without the food, the dog would unlearn the association and eventually no longer salivate. This part of the experiment was referred to as the "extinction process." As with Pavlov's dogs, the effects of negative conditioning on people can be reversed as well. Our goal is to first identify the areas in life where choice has been subjugated and then introduce the method to eradicate its influence. Your association with negative conditioning is headed for extinction, and the results could be the most liberating experience of your life.

There are many aspects of our lives that go unnoticed and enter our consciousness only when they are intentionally explored. Consider this: If there were no such thing as water, we would have no fear of drowning. Obviously, water exists and we've had to learn how to adapt to it. Acquiring the skill to swim provides belief and negates the fear. The same is true for negative conditioning. It surrounds us every day. The sooner we learn to identify it, the better equipped we will be to overcome it.

Let's begin with our early years. As mentioned before, negative conditioning becomes a part of our lives as soon as we're able to communicate. From the moment we begin to understand speech, we're bombarded with negative responses to a myriad of issues in our lives. A rather unsettling finding backs this up:

"The average 2-year-old hears 436 negative comments per day, compared to just 34 positive ones."

University of Iowa

It's easy to see how imbalanced the influences on a child's life can become. The sheer numbers alone are staggering. If we use the figures from the study above, in just one year the average 2-year-old will hear almost 160,000 negative comments, compared with just over 12,000 positive ones. This imbalance will certainly begin to have an effect on a child's sense of what's possible and what's not. In essence it begins to subvert their belief system.

Fortunately, at this age a child's resolve is strong because of the innate instinct to not give up. Self-limiting behavior is something that's learned, not inherited. If we were born with this behavior, we would never have the persistence to learn to walk or talk or learn physical coordination. With the thousands of repetitions necessary through trial and error, mastering these skills wouldn't be possible without absolute determination and an unwavering belief system. This instinctive determination can usually overcome a child's excess of negative conditioning for a number of years. The child will usually stay strong and still trust that anything is possible. As we get older, however, the cumulative affect of negative conditioning will begin to challenge our belief systems. We will begin to wonder if we can. The negatives pile on top of the negatives until a belief begins to transition to a doubt.

As we move from childhood into our teenage years, we bring with us more than a decade of negative baggage. In addition, the negative conditioning begins to take on a more serious tone. The burden on our psyche now carries much more weight than it did when we were children because we are also being told that our actions have consequences.

It's a testament to the human spirit that, throughout our teen years, a small percentage will retain the resolve to believe in their dreams and disregard the input of society. However, the majority of teens begin to accept the possibility of "can't" and shift the paradigm of their belief systems accordingly. This shift can have a lifelong impact. What happens is, there's a shift from society's believing that your dreams are not possible to *you* believing the same. When this occurs, it's the beginning of the development of self-limiting behavior.

Reaction to the years of society's input varies greatly from one person to another. By the time a teenager enters early adulthood, he may have completely shut off his internal mechanism that allows him to dream and believe. Others may still hold on to their dreams but will begin to shield them from their family and peers for fear of ridicule. Picture your belief system in the form of photographs taken at various stages of your life.

Some are bright and clear, while others are faded and tattered. If you still get excited about the thought of studying dinosaurs but you're internal voice begins to parrot society's reasons why you will probably fail, your dream begins to fade. The older you get, the more these reasons sound logical and the more you may adopt them as your own.

As we make the transition from our teen years to early adulthood, the cumulative effect of negative conditioning combines with the pressures of personal responsibility. This combination can prove lethal. These responsibilities occur in a number of areas of life that are completely foreign to us. For the first time, our responsibilities may extend into relationships, financial commitments, post-secondary education and employment. The new forms of negative conditioning relating to these areas begin to sound more and more convincing.

The natural reaction to all these new pressures is to move toward the area of least resistance, which is closer to accepting the status quo and further from our passion. Once the door closes on our teen years, these responsibilities appear to become very real.

The vast majority of young adults lose focus on their dreams because they're too consumed by dealing with day-to-day responsibilities and worrying about tomorrow. It's much easier at this point to simply let our dreams fade to black. Having a passion has now been replaced with having a boss.

The final phase of life where we deal with negative conditioning is our adult years. Most of us enter this phase in our late twenties or early thirties. By this time, formal education is well behind us and our careers are centered primarily on meeting financial and family obligations. By now the cumulative effect of negative conditioning has built a virtual library of reasons of why we can't in our minds. We no longer even need the input of society to provide the reasons that we shouldn't follow our dreams. Our mind is now able to produce a litany of reasons on its own, from memory. As mentioned at the beginning of this chapter, the ultimate danger of negative conditioning is the creation of self-limiting behavior. By this stage in life for most the process is all but complete.

The final impediment to pursuing our life's passion is guilt. If a lifetime of negative conditioning hasn't been enough to deter us from following our passions, society is only too glad to pull out the guilt card. By the time we reach this stage in our lives, there's a very real level of achievement and responsibility to others that we will be forced to consider. We of oftentimes reminded of how fortunate we are and should not ask for more.

As a young adult you may still have an ember inside you that flickers for your once-great passion, but society is quick to put it out to stem the flames. What happens is that every time you consider or mention your passion, those around you remind you of everything you should be thankful for. This causes you to again doubt your passion. You're also told over and over not to wish for more than you have and are constantly reminded of how many people would love to trade places with you. At this point, you will likely have a moment of thankfulness and return to your current life. Far too many seem to be destined to continue on the same path and lead what we're told is "a good life." Sadly, it's just not the one we're capable or deserving of.

Before moving on to other areas of negative conditioning, it's important for you to know that this is not the endgame. You're beginning to get a clear understanding of negative conditioning at various stages in life and may be feeling overwhelmed by how familiar it all sounds to you. But the key to overcoming negative conditioning is in recognizing that it truly is only a mental perception. The ability to find your passion and live your dreams is where it has always been, right there inside you. In subsequent chapters, you'll learn how to overcome the effects of negative conditioning at any stage of life and erase your self-limiting behavior.

"You don't drown by falling in the water;

you drown by staying there."

Edwin Louis Cole

A few years ago, I learned of a lesson taught by a psychology professor. On the first day of the semester, the professor walked into the lecture hall and put his books and papers on the lectern. Without saying a word, he picked up a piece of chalk and walked to the blackboard. On it he wrote, "2 + 2 = 4." He set the chalk down and turned to the students. After surveying the crowd for a moment, he again went to the chalkboard and wrote on it, "2 + 2 = 4". He again put down his chalk and turned to the students. With new determination, the professor tapped firmly on the board, *"2 + 2 = 4."* He slapped the chalk back into its place on the shelf at the bottom of the chalkboard and turned to glare at the students in the hall. They began to fidget in their seats but remained silent. Finally the professor returned to the board, picked up the chalk and wrote, *"2 + 2 = 5."* He put the chalk down and turned to the class. By the time he'd turned back around, a number of students had put up their hands. He pointed to a girl in the front row and said, *"Yes, miss?"* *"Sir, two plus two does not equal five, that's wrong"* she said. With that the professor looked at the class and simply said, *"Isn't that interesting? Three times I got it right and not one person said a thing. Once I get it wrong and you can't wait to jump on me. Class dismissed."* What a brilliant lesson.

This constant focus on our mistakes rather than our accomplishments is another aspect of negative conditioning that's responsible for chipping away at our self-belief system. Examples of focusing on our mistakes are everywhere. They happen to us as children at school, in sport, at work and at home with our families. We've become conditioned to count how many we get wrong and have made that the measure of our endeavors.

> *"Keep away from people who try to belittle your ambitions.*
>
> *Small people always do that, but the really great make you*
>
> *feel that you, too, can become great."*
>
> Mark Twain, American author, humorist

Take a moment and think about who should decide what is and what isn't grown-up. How you live your life is neither childish nor grown-up; it's simply your life. There's a great story about a singer songwriter's early days and the challenges he faced. When he was in his late teens, his father once said in front of him to company at their home, *"He fancies himself a singer. It's time he grew up and got a job and learned some responsibility."* If that young man by the name of Reginald Dwight hadn't had the strength to overcome negative conditioning, the world would have never felt the passion *of "Don't Let the Sun Go Down on Me."*

"Great spirits have always encountered

violent opposition from mediocre minds."

Albert Einstein, American physicist

Before you're too hard on Elton John's father, consider what our education system is doing to rob today's youths of their passion and their rightful place in the world. When my oldest son, Justin, was finishing up his final year of high school, the colleges and universities put on an evening forum. They were looking to woo hot new prospects into their halls of hallowed learning. Toward the end of one presentation, the moderator asked the roughly 60 students on hand which ones had decided on career paths. When I looked around, two had put up their hands. I was shocked.

That evening created a spark that lit the fire. I was a long way from finishing this philosophy, but standing there that night, I realized just how few children today are being guided and encouraged to follow their passions and their dreams. With hundreds of thousands of students being herded through the system every year, it became apparent that this was a recipe for failure.

Every year, students are pushed through the system with little or no regard for what it is that they would like to do or what they have a passion for. These students enter college or university with no real direction or purpose, no idea why they're there in the first place. They are simply reminded constantly from all areas of society that they have to go. They've been told hundreds or perhaps thousands of times that if they don't get a good education, there will be consequences.

Throughout a child's life the conversation goes something like this. Young Bobby asks,

"What should I do"?

The world replies, *"You need to get a good........................ education".*

The child responds as all children do with *"Sure but.............. why"?*

The world tells him, *"Well Bobby, if you don't get a good education you won't be able to get.............. a good job".*

"O.K." says Bobby, *"But................. why"?*

"Well" says the world *"If you don't get a good job you won't be able to ....pay your bills and support your family and pay your taxes and be a responsible member of society"*

To which Bobby replies, *"Oh, I think I have it now. Let me make sure I have this correct. So what you are telling me is that you want me to go to school doing something I won't enjoy so that I will one day be able to get a job I don't enjoy and do that for the rest of my life. Do I have it right"?*

"Yes Bobby" says the world. *"You have it right".*

Ah, there it is. The big stick of society warning that if you don't heed its advice, fire and brimstone will rain down from the heavens. Young people are told that if they don't swim upstream with the rest, they can expect a mediocre labor-intensive life at best. The carrot that's dangled in front of them is the idea that with a post-secondary education, the world will be their oyster. The problem is that through all of this, almost no one bothers to say, *"Tell us your passion and we'll help you get there"*.

As society, we may decide to fix the education system when we one day realize that students without passion will never truly reach their potential. The current education system reminds us of mice caught in a maze. If a mouse is put into a maze in total darkness, it will wander in circles for a while and soon give up and die. If, on the other hand, a faint light is visible in the distance, the mouse will push itself well beyond its normal physical capacity. We're like the mice. If we're given a purpose or a chance to reach our destination, we'll show extraordinary resolve.

> *"Far better is it to dare mighty things, to win glorious triumphs, even though checkered by failure, ... than to rank with those poor spirits who neither enjoy much nor suffer much, because they live in a gray twilight that knows not victory nor defeat."*
> Theodore Roosevelt, 26th president of the United States

The normal course of action for students today goes something like this: They complete high school and talk to the guidance counselor once or twice about what jobs they may be suited for and where the best prospects for money are. After that, they sit down with their parents and decide on a course of action based on tuition, location and overall scholastic record. Once this decision is made, these young people then split into four distinct categories. The first three are an indication of what's wrong with our society.

1. Those in the first group drop out of school. There's been talk recently about revamping this term to something like *non-completion students*. The logic is that by referring to students as dropouts, it stigmatizes them and creates perpetual problems for them in society. What should be of greater concern is that millions of young people are wandering through life without direction or passion.

The students who don't complete post-secondary education are the thin edge of the wedge and clearly represent what's wrong with the system. The latest statistics show this to be the largest group: Of the students entering post-secondary education, 49.1% did not complete the term.

Ask yourself why. Is it because half the population is incapable or mentally challenged or drug addicts and alcoholics? Quite simply it's because these people had no motivation going in. They had no reason, no burning desire, no light at the end of the tunnel to push them and keep them going. As a result, the balance tipped in favor of giving up. The prospect of studying, attending lectures, completing homework assignments and pushing themselves to succeed every day had no appeal because there was no goal to be achieved other than some vague edict from society and their parents that they should. They were never able to hold on to the notion that *"if you succeed at this, you will be able to become that."*

This group of people in fact *will* be stigmatized by society because they don't hold that piece of paper. Most will go through life moving from one job to the next. They'll achieve varying levels of success as defined by society (stable job, decent income, responsible position), but few will ever know what it's like to live their dreams. Some may actually toy with the idea of their dreams in the future, and a very few may be fortunate enough to set life aside and do what's necessary to achieve that. For most, however, the reality of their situation, expenses, families and the pressures of society will keep them chained to the path of responsibility. This group will continue to *"do the right thing"* and stay the course in lives that pay the bills but do little to fulfill their personal journeys.

2. The second group is those who finish a post-secondary education that's unrelated to anything they're passionate about. These people will eventually go on to other education further down the road in pursuit of their real passion.

These are the people who did everything right according to society's model. They focused on where the good jobs were. They put in the effort, sat at the lectures, completed the assignments, gave up a social life, worked one or two part-time jobs to get themselves through.

This group made it to graduation; only to realize that this wasn't the ticket to ride they'd been led to believe. Their magical diplomas unquestionably qualified them to fill in the appropriate boxes on job applications. And these were the jobs that they were told would be waiting and would hold the key to their future. The problem was that the jobs they were now qualified for weren't part of their personal journey. They didn't have a passion for what they were educated to do. As a result, the work didn't come easily to them. One of the most profound quotes I've ever heard came from an unlikely source, comedian Steve Martin. He said, *"You gotta wanna."* I've never heard it put better.

It's like the chemistry between a man and a woman, between best friends or business partners. And prospective employers can sense it. Whether you "wanna" will not be evident in your resume, but will show up in your interview or your performance on the job. In more cases than not, it's the deal-breaker.

Those who are able to find work in a field related to their education will leave feeling strangely unfulfilled. They'll struggle with their place in the grand scheme of things. They'll question why it is that they aren't satisfied with a life that, on the surface, they should be very grateful for. Along the way, they will question their lives enough to come to the conclusion that they want more.

This group will take on the task of changing ships in midstream. They'll walk away from the life so carefully crafted by society and do what it takes to follow their passion. What these people will go through will be extraordinary. Many of these people will have been in the workplace for a number of years. They will have developed a lifestyle, obligations, debts and habits and taken on dependents. They'll face sacrifice, compromise, hard work and doubt. In many cases, they will have to convince not only themselves of the worthiness of this new endeavor but family members and those who have come to count on them.

That said, these people are the fortunate ones. They will succeed. Their lives will change, and they will go on to develop a new sense of purpose and take their rightful place in the world. If they had admitted their passion early on or were encouraged to follow their dreams before all these obligations became a reality, the road they could have traveled would have been smooth and fast. What road? The road that exists for them now. I suspect you may very well fall into this group. Be aware that it takes no superhuman abilities to join this group. The simple reality is that you're here and you want to be there. The rewards will be great if you do what is necessary and spend the rest of your life doing what moves you and makes you smile. This statement holds true for us all. *"Live today because there will never be another today."*

3. The third group is those who finish society's prescribed course of education and never use it. Because of obligations, they feel unable to go back to school or learn a new skill that would fulfill their dreams. This group is the saddest, I believe. This group did everything right according to the pressures of society. Like thelast group, this one studied, worked the part-time jobs, attended the lectures, incurred the debt and walked away with diplomas. This group, because of lack of belief that they can change, will find employment not in the field they were educated for but in a totally unrelated field. Because of their perception of responsibilities, specific situations and self-limitation, they will never see the way to re-invent themselves.

One of the reasons these people stay the course is, again, society's conditioning. These people are admired in life. They are the solid citizens. They are the mothers and fathers who always did the right thing. They always put their loved ones and co-workers and friends ahead of themselves. They have succeeded in convincing themselves that this was what life was supposed to be. They move from job to job effortlessly, chasing the prize of financial stability and job security. In quiet times by themselves, while driving the car, walking the dog or staring out the window at work, they will briefly entertain the thought that there should be something more. Then that voice in their head, the voice of society, will remind them that they should be satisfied with everything they have. It tells them they should be humbled to live such an existence. They will be reminded that there are millions of people who would trade places with them in a second. After a moment or two of self-indulgence, they snap out of it and go back to being responsible, doing the right thing, feeling just a bit small for wanting something more than society had seen fit to deliver. The daydream passes, and with it, their passion is pushed aside one more time.

4. The final group is what appears to most to be the chosen ones. They are the people who know exactly what their passion is, are totally unaffected by what others think of their choice and seek out the education or training to fulfill their dream. This group is by far the smallest and most elite. Of great importance you should understand that there is no real or physical reason why so few follow this path. There's no question that these people are the true winners of the prize of life.

These people had the good fortune and personal strength to set aside the voices that told us all to go this way or that. When these people entered post-secondary education or whatever form of training they chose (it could be working on a farm learning to milk cows if that was their dream), the vision of achieving their dreams was firmly set in their minds. They were able connect the effort to the reward and welcomed the journey with great enthusiasm. They were able to put forth whatever effort was required because it allowed them to live their dream.

The people in this group will go on to lead extraordinary lives. They will be centered, focused, happy, fulfilled and successful. Certainly, there are no guarantees in life, but this group is beginning with a huge advantage. They're more likely to be great employees, fathers, mothers, co-workers, citizens and contributing members of society. So much pressure is put on all of us to be responsible, to go where the jobs are and to *"think about your future."* The simple truth is that if you do something you love, you will see it as your passion and to you it will never be just a job. The ultimate end result then will be a society that has benefited greatly.

It's easy to be great at something you love. I'm often reminded of the guy who mumbles and groans to get out of bed for work all week long but pops up at 5 a.m. to go golfing on the weekends. This group is like the golfer. The people who live with passion pop out of bed every morning with great expectations of the day before them. Because of this, they will outperform most and will be recognized and rewarded for their efforts. The key for these people is that they will never look upon what they do as an effort. It's a passion. It's their personal journey. They will consistently "Look Forward to Mondays".

To outsiders, it appears that these people have some exceptional gift. They appear to breeze through their education or training where others struggle and toil. The key is not a special gift but rather a purpose. When given a purpose, anyone can accomplish incredible feats.

When you consider those who are in the first three categories, the costs just in terms of education are staggering. Here in North America we spend, on average, over $20,000 per student for each year they're in the educational system. This equates to $280,000. per student just to prepare them for post-secondary education. It's astonishing when you think that all this money is being spent while so little effort is directed toward helping students discover the fuel that will propel them to success. The system could be invaluable in helping them get the education to achieve and realize their passion. It's the only thing that can keep them stimulated and interested for a lifetime. It's what will bring them self-fulfillment and, in turn, make them a valuable member of society.

So far we have discussed only the financial cost. The human cost is immeasurable. There's no price you can put on a fulfilled, happy, meaningful life. Obviously, for this to become the norm, we would have to shift the paradigm of the education system in society. This is philosophically exciting to talk about but functionally unsound. There is something you can do as an individual, however. You can adopt this philosophy right now, today, and make the changes in your own life that elude the vast majority and their children. While the majority of people reading this book may be well beyond their school years, it's important to recognize where our limitations originated and to identify what it was that brought us to where we are today. To reach a destination, knowing where you came from will allow you to plot a course correction.

> Jim Rohn once said, *"What happens, happens to us all. Its what we do with what happens that determines the people we become"*.

The negative conditioning you have endured throughout your life to this point is as common as raindrops. It happens to us all. Where we next will go is to shine the light on the fact that you can do something about it. What the intake of all this negative information has done is to create behaviors. As we learned from Pavlov, what can be created can be eliminated. Before that, the story of a boy named Mattie.

My name is Mattie

The following story is one of the most remarkable and touching stories of a life I've ever known. It proves every theory of what's possible in life and what can be accomplished in a very short length of time. Rather than write his life story, I've decided to reprint a short autobiography written by Mattie himself.

"My name is Mattie Joseph Thaddeus Stepanek (my real name is Mathew, but I like Mattie). I am almost 11 years old, and I home-school doing a high school curriculum. I began writing when I was about 3 years old, and now have a collection that contains thousands of poems, dozens of essays and short stories, and many illustrations. I have even bound some of my books at home, and a bound anthology of my writing was presented to the Library of Congress during the fall of 2000. I have also won many awards for my writing, including the Melinda A Lawrence International Book Award in 1999 for "most inspirational work."

I have a rare form of muscular dystrophy called mitochondrial myopathy, and I also have something called dysautonomia. That means that my "automatic" systems, like breathing, heart rate, body temperature, oxygenation, digestion and things like that, don't always work well on their own.

So I use extra oxygen all the time, and when I am tired of sleeping, I use a ventilator that breathes for me and some other machines, too. I also use a power wheelchair much of the time to save energy and move my medical equipment around. My two brothers and one sister died during childhood from the same thing I have, and my mother uses a power wheelchair all the time because she has the adult form of this disability.

I love to read, write and do public speaking at conferences and seminars. This year I was chosen to be the Maryland goodwill ambassador for the Muscular Dystrophy Association. I get to participate in many fundraising events that will help find a cure for neuromuscular diseases, and support children and families in celebrating life during the time before a cure is found. I also enjoy playing with Legos, drawing, Pokemon, and studying about famous people and the martial arts (I have earned a 1st degree black belt in a Korean art similar to tae kwon do).

When I grow up, I want to be a peacemaker. My biggest role model for this is Jimmy Carter, who has been a wonderful peanut farmer, politician, and peacemaker. I call him the "perfect hero." I would like to work as a mediator and share my poetry, essays, and philosophy with others so that they may be inspired to work with other people, too. I want people to know that in every life there are storms. But we must remember to play after every storm and to celebrate the gift of life as we have it, or else life becomes a task, rather than a gift. We must always listen to the song in our heart, and share that song with others.

Mattie lost his battle with MD on June 22, 2004, at the age of 13. During the early years of his life, he'd decided to set three very lofty goals: He wanted to write a book, meet Oprah Winfrey and former President Jimmy Carter. He did everything he set out to do and much more. He didn't write just one book but eight and had two on the *New York Times* best-seller list. He didn't just meet Oprah Winfrey -- they became friends and he was a regular guest on her show, inspiring millions. And finally, he didn't simply meet his mentor, former President Carter -- they, too, became friends and worked on world-peace plans together.

Mattie's strength and belief in life were summed up in one of his poems.

On Being a Champion

A champion is a winner,

A hero . . .

Someone who never gives up

Even when the going gets rough.

A champion is a member of

A winning team . . .

Someone who overcomes challenges

Even when it requires creative solutions.

A champion is an optimist,

A hopeful spirit . . .

Someone who plays the game,

Even when the game is called life.

There can be a champion in each of us,

If we live as a winner,

If we live as a member of the team,

If we live with a hopeful spirit,

For life.

Examples of courage and hope and pursuing that sense of wonder surround us every day. Hope springs eternal from children like Mattie. Simply because they believe they can. We were the winner every day that he was here with us.

4

The science of human behavior

The entire purpose of this book is to provide the structure and disciplines necessary to have the life you are deserving of. In order to reach your goals and live with the passion, there are aspects of your current behaviors that will need to be altered and refined to make it happen. One of the cornerstones to accomplishing what you set out to do is to change certain behaviors. Have you ever wondered why it is that you act a certain way or find it difficult to stick to something and can't seem to change? Altering and improving the behaviors that are holding you back is absolutely necessary to allow you to achieve your goal to live with passion. Changing negative behaviors is required for us all so that we may open the doors that for decades may have remained shut. As Jim Rohn once said, *"In order to have more you must become more"*. The more in this case is to improve and refine the behaviors that will make this journey possible.

Human behavior is greatly rooted in science and I have found it to be one of the most effective tools I have in helping my clients achieve their goals. What we are going to discussed is completely science based and will help you gain a clear understanding and thus motivate you to invest in the activity necessary to create change. Behaviors are pre-set actions and reactions linked to and based upon past experiences and the psychological baggage that accompanies them. These ingrained behaviors allow us all to carry forward unforeseen obstacles into our lives.

What I want you to know from this moment on is that there is nothing wrong with *you*. It is quite common to *"own"* the issues surrounding negative behaviors. Know this. If there is something that I currently struggle with there is nothing wrong with me. I was born perfect and so were you. What may be wrong stems from negative behaviors created from thousands of experiences you have had in life. It is the exposure to the experiences of life that creates the behaviors that hold us back. If I were to hang the blame of a negative behavior on myself and say, *"There is something wrong with me"*, then I am beaten and cannot alter the behavior. I can't change who I am as a person. If however I accept the truth that it was the experiences that I was surrounded by that created the negative behaviors then I am able to clearly identify and invest in the changes necessary. The answer to begin to change is to alter the information you have taken in and in effect begin to overwrite files in the sub-conscious mind that contain the blocks of your potential.

The core reason why most do not live an authentic life and achieve their goals is due to the impact of the intake of negative information over a sustained period of time. Negative sub-conscious imprinting over many years begins to create doubt and is the wall divides success and failure. The reality of what is possible is rooted in a question that I pose to almost every audience I speak to. Here is it; *"If you set a goal, find out what is necessary to achieve it, begin to invest in the activity and you don't stop, is most any goal achievable*'? The resounding answer every time is, *"Yes, if you followed that philosophy then most any goal is achievable".* To which I reply. *"Gotchya! You just told me that you could have anything you want if you don't stop".* Looking around the room each and every time I see the bewilderment in the eyes of those around me. That quiet resignation of the statement sinks in and they realize just how simple the process is and how much they have denied themselves over the years. They failed quite simply because they stopped. They ceased the forward motion that was essential to achieving their goal.

This is the one aspect of human behavior that fascinates me more than any other. If the absolute truth about this statement, *"If we set a goal, find out what's necessary to achieve it, begin and don't stop any goal is attainable"* is true, and it is, then what is it exactly that stops us from doing what we know would produce the prize? Let's look at a very basic example of this. Lets say that my goal was to walk across the room. In order to achieve any goal I would have to take stock of where I was and research what would be necessary to achieve it. And so I do. I find out the only mode of transport I have is walking, so I begin taking the necessary steps to cross the room. On the way however I begin to encounter issues. There are a number of toys left on the floor by the children that I have to walk around. I start worrying about how long this will take and if dinner will be ready on time. I get side tracked by the downturn in the economy and the client who cancelled and all of the pitfalls I did not anticipate when I set out. About half way across the room I start to think that I should have been much further and begin to question whether this is working or not. I begin to doubt if success is possible. These doubts build up and build up until eventually I stop. I cease any forward motion. I have decided it is not working and so I stop and that I am never taking another step. Based on this scenario, my goal has now become unachievable. If I had kept walking in spite of the challenges and setbacks I would most certainly have reached the other side of the room but now I never will because I stopped.

Given that my goal or any goal is absolutely attainable lets examine what happened. The question must be *"What stopped me"*? Was it the toys strewn on the floor? Was it the challenge of the economy? Was it the concern that dinner may be late? The answer is a resounding no. None of these challenges were insurmountable and I was able to get past each one. Here is what stopped me. A thought! As I said, this facet of human behavior fascinates me more than anything. When we boil all of this down I find out that what caused me to stop was little more than a thought. A thought that I should have been further along. A thought that I didn't anticipate the toys or economy or any other challenges. O.K. then. Where did the thought come from? Thought as you know is not something we are born with. Tabula Rasa is Latin for the term black slate which describes our psychological state when we come into this world. Thought then is something created after birth. Here is the process.

- ➤ Thought begins as the intake of information through experience
- ➤ This information is stored in a cluster of cells in the brain called a neuronet.
- ➤ The retrieval of this information through a neuropathway comes forward as a thought

> Thought then is nothing more than the retrieval of information based on past a experience that is no longer here. We an overcome a thought

When we examine the process of thought we can then easily see that the thought that stops our activity is little more than the recall of stored information based on an incident or experience that is no longer here. In essence it is a hologram of an experience from the past that steals away the absolute majority of goals. It is critical to understand this process. It is the stopping, not the obstacle that negates the process of forward motion. When moving forward through the process of achieving your life vision it is essential to understand that the greatest challenge you will ever overcome is the voice in your head. Understanding what it is and how it is created greatly diminishes its power.

Now lets delve into the science of the process. First of all I want you to be impressed with yourself. Gaining an understanding for what you have at your disposal is key. Lets start with the human brain. You do not lack the capacity to think, learn, become or create anything possible. Your brain is comprised of some 100 billion brain cells or neurons. More cells than there are stars in the Milky Way. On the exterior cell wall of every cell are synapses, which in affect are the wiring mechanism that allow one cell to talk to the other. Each cell has between 1,000-10,000 synapses on it. Based on these facts we can then determine that the human brain has the calculating power of the following number. 100 billion to the power of one to ten thousand! Even the function of the small brain of a bird landing on a branch in the wind would take the most powerful supercomputer days to compute, if it were possible at all. A bird does it in seconds. The power of our brain is almost beyond comprehension. From the outset you should be impressed with your capabilities and potential and know that you have all that you need to accomplish anything you could set out to do.

Now that you have an appreciation for how powerful your brain is, this now sets the stage to beginning to understand how it works. As you now know the intake of information over a sustained period of time is what is responsible for creating our belief system. Just the findings from the study of 2 year olds from the University of Iowa uncovered the nearly 160,000 negative impressions they received every year certainly proves this out. As this information is taken in, it is stored in the sub-conscious mind. The actual functional storage unit within the brain is called a neuronet. A neuronet is a small cluster of cells in the brain held together with the synapses. The first time a piece of information is taken in the number of cells in the cluster is extremely small. A simple explanation is to think of each neuronet as representing a thought or action or the memory of a piece of information. What makes each of us uniquely different is that we have all formed different neuronets based on the experiences we have throughout life.

If I were to tell you during casual conversation that I drive a black car you would in all likelihood not recall that information in a day or two. The reason being that the storage unit for this information would be so small it would be almost impossible to retrieve it. If however I were to get you cell phone number and call you every day for two to three months and say, *"Hi, this is Randy I drive a black car"* and hang up, within a couple of months it would no longer be necessary for me to call or to be anywhere near you. Someone would merely mention the words black car and you would instantly think two things. One Randy. Two annoying! The access of this information would be so easy now due to the repetitive input. What happens is that every time the information is input, the neuronet grows in size and allows for the information to be much more easily retrieved.

We can see that this process of the intake of information and its storage provides great advantage for the process of learning. As we study and take in information relative to knowledge we want to acquire or a skill we want to develop it serves us well. If however the information taken in and stored in a neuronet guides us in the wrong direction it can become a hindrance. The process is this. If you do something once, a lose connection is formed. Do it again and again and again and it builds a stronger connection. The result of the repetitive action is that the information becomes more readily accessible from our sub-conscious.

The storage of this information, both good and bad affects us on a minute-by-minute basis throughout our entire lives. What happens is that the storage of this information is the cross-reference library for all thought and action. Every thought we have and every action we engage in is cross-referenced in a millisecond with the sub-conscious mind. As an example, when I am eating a plate of pasta and bring the fork up to my mouth, if I notice steam coming off of it I then go inside my brain to cross reference the information from past experience relative to this experience. When I do this the brain says, *"Blow on it dummy, you burned your mouth the last time"*. One final point is to think of the storage of information inside your brain like a filing system. When we are having a new experience or thought and go inside the sub-conscious mind to cross-reference what we know about it we grab the top file. The top file in each case would be the largest neuronet relative to that particular thought or experience.

I see clear evidence of this process again and again with the major corporations I provide coaching programs for. It is remarkable. You will see two individuals within the company in a sales position. Both work for the exact same company. Both had identical training. Both have identical access to the consumer market. Both have been with the company for an identical period of time. Here is where the similarity ends. One is earning $25,000. a year and the other $150,000. Many would wonder how this disparity is possible. This is all relative to the information stored in the files of their respective sub-conscious minds. Remember, as we all have different experiences in life, we all have different information stored in the files. One of the key activities of any sales associate is to book meetings using the telephone. Here is an example of what happens. The first associate earning $25,000. a year picks up the phone to make a call. As with all thought and action he or she cross-references what they know about the process with the sub-conscious mind. Think of all information as being stored in separate file folders. When the folder is opened that contains the information about calling new clients the cross-reference tells the associate that this does not work for them. The information in this file says that this doesn't work and as a result he's broke. Considering the information provided, how do you think the call turns out if it's made at all? The second associate earning $150,000. a year picks up the phone and opens the file in his sub-conscious mind. The information contained in his file says this is an exciting process, meets wonderful people and books meetings with interested prospects everyday. His file says that this is a direct line to his bank account. Go. Based upon this cross-reference of information, how do you think the call turns out? The answer is pretty well. That's one of the primary reasons he's earning $150,000. a year because the information stores in the sub-conscious mind is supportive of the activity.

I hope you can see how the correlation to the incorrect information stored in your sub-conscious mind can have such a detrimental affect on the success of action. In effect what we need to do then is to change the information in the files that contain the incorrect information. These are the files that are responsible for creating negative outcomes.

Here's the good news. Formerly, this statement was believed to be true, "*You can't teach an old dog new tricks*". The consensus in the scientific community was that information in our brains became somewhat hard wired and could not be altered. It has now been proven scientifically that not only can the storage of information be altered but that under the right conditions brain cells continue to grow and IQ can actually increase as we age.

What science has now discovered is that the connections formed within a neuronet will break down if they are no longer used over a sustained period of time. The process is referred to as neuroplasticity. This term relates to the scientific discovery of the dissolving and re-forming of neuronets. As a result new neuronets can be formed from the repetitive action of a new thought or activity.

A great example of a large neuronet would be that apples are round and red. Just imagine how many times that information has been input into the sub-conscious mind creating the corresponding neuronet? Since we are old enough to begin to communicate, the support of this piece of information was everywhere. Apples are in grocery stores and on trees, books, television and conversation. As a result of the input of this information over and over again it has become deeply wired into our sub-conscious mind. If however, for the next several months apples being round and red ceased to exist we would no longer input the information that apples are round and red. As of this moment apples are square and blue. Over time the connection relating to red and round would begin to dissolve and would be replaced by the image and perceived belief that apples are square and blue. After a period of 2-3 months if you entered a grocery store, your sub-conscious mind would survey the produce counter searching for square blue apples. You would put them into a bag, pay for them and go home and you would have altered one of the strongest neuronets in your brain. Even the most dominant neuronets that we have can be altered.

While the science involved in altering the information in the sub-conscious mind and ultimately behavior may be very complicated, the process itself is actually very simple. When the steps are outlined as to how to accomplish this and change behavior I often get the standard response, *"Oh come on, that can't possibly work. It's too simple"*. My answer every time is this. *"How do you think the information got in your sub-conscious in the first place"?* The answer is through the repetitive input from information input from the world around us over a sustained period of time. The process to alter the information in the files is exactly the same process, only the input is through intentional repetitive action. If we take in information over and over it causes this new neuronet to grow in size, making it more and more accessible. Conversely, if the old file containing the incorrect information is no longer accessed over a sustained period of time, the synapses will begin to dissolve and the neuronet will begin to shrink in size. Following this process over a period of 2-3 months, the top file that originally contained the incorrect information will be replaced by the new information that serves you and directs you to invest in positive actions and activities. This change will lead to you making completely different decisions based on the information accessed. The outcome of this will lead to a change in behavior and ultimately the creation of a positive result.

Again, changing negative behaviors will be an essential element in the process of being able to accomplish your goal once defined and will assist you to become one of those who are living the life they are deserving of. The exercise to accomplish this will be at the end of this chapter titled, *"Reprogramming Exercise"*. It will only take only a few minutes a day but will require your commitment on a daily basis to repeat it often enough to produce the necessary results and engrain the correct information. When setting out on this journey it is important to understand the definition of commitment, *"The continuation of an activity in the apparent absence of results"*. Write this down and keep it with you. It will serve you on the days when that voice in your head is nagging *"where is it"?* Now that we have covered how the intake, storage and retrieval of information affects current and future decisions and ultimately results, we will now move on to one of the most fascinating elements of human behavior. The chemistry of the mystery.

"There is nothing either good non bad but thinking makes it so"

William Shakespeare

Man has long pondered the question, *"I don't know why I keep doing what I am doing when I know it is wrong?"* Recently during a group coaching session a client asked the question; *"I changed my activity, began getting a positive result and then stopped. Why?"* I think this is something that we can all relate to and experience many times over life. Even though we are going to the gym and our muscles are growing. Even thought we are eating better and the numbers on the scale are going in the right direction. Even though we are getting more business by contacting more clients, it is an often-experienced phenomenon of human behavior that we stop. The answer relates to how behaviors are formed on a bio-chemical level and how change comes about. What happens is that when we begin a new activity, the action is being driven from a conscious mind perspective. We are in effect *"making"* ourselves do it. True change in behavior comes about when thought or action is driven by the sub-conscious mind. From a position of calculation the proof is clear. The sub-conscious mind processes information at a rate hundreds of times faster than the conscious mind.

The process of transferring a thought or action from a conscious mind perspective to sub-conscious will take between 2-3 months of repeating it daily to achieve this shift. A good example that I note often in sessions and seminars is to look around the room and see that all the men have shaved and all the women have done their hair and put on their make-up. I ask the question, *"Do you remember doing it this morning"?* The simple answer is we really don't. Rarely would you see a man pacing around his home in the morning repeating over and over again, *"Don't forget to shave. Don't forget to shave".* When a behavior makes the transfer from being controlled by the conscious to the sub-conscious mind this stress is removed and we invest in the activity on autopilot. The objective then to create any new behavior is to repeat the thought or activity often enough. Until this is accomplished, reversion back to old behaviors is inevitable.

Previously, it was believed that it was laziness or a flawed personality that stops so many of us from being able to achieve our dreams. What we now know is that our internal chemistry and a very complicated scientific process play a critical role. The human body is the greatest pharmaceutical factory in the world. Our bodies are capable of producing any drug or chemical compound known to mankind. Whatever the medical world can produce as an external drug or stimulant, our bodies have the capacity to produce internally and do.

For decades science speculated that there was a chemical connection between emotions and behavior but they couldn't find it. What was driving science was that there was more to an emotion than the psychological side. They knew that there was also a physical component to all emotions. As an example if you were to step onto a street looking in one direction and heard screeching tires behind you what emotion would you have? Fear? Terror? Now along with the psychological shock and thought of *"I'm going to die"* there are physical manifestations going on as well. Your heart would race. Your hands would shake. Your knees would become weak. It was this physical response that science believed proved that there was a chemical link between emotions and behavior but they could not find it. Finally, Dr. Candice Pert, the lead researcher on the project broke the code. She was able to unveil the process of the chemical link by discovering the brain's opiate receptors and proving the connection between emotions and behavior. This research opened the door to explain so much about human behavior.

What they discovered is that each emotion produces it's own chemical compound or neuropeptide. These chemicals, it was discovered are produced in a tiny organ inside the brain called the hypothalamus. These are the chemicals that prepare the body for action. The process of what happens is this. We have an emotion. The hypothalamus produces the chemical compound or neuropeptide. These then are released and are circulated throughout the body. On the exterior wall of every cell in our bodies are cell receptors. There are thousands of receptors on the wall of every cell and each receptor is designed to intake only one chemical compound. I often describe the receptors as a keyhole. My key would not start your car and yours would not start mine. These receptors provide the chemicals or neuropeptides a place to dock onto the cell and allow the chemical compound to enter. One of these neuropeptides you may be familiar with is called endorphins and is linked to what we refer to as the "runner's high." The neuropetides created from emotions are referred to as MOE'S or molecules of emotion. These chemicals are responsible for the physical feelings related to emotions. It is the physical state we enter resulting from anger, happiness, sadness, depression, elation, fear etc.

Our cell receptors receive chemicals in two ways; either internally or externally.

Exogenous-are chemicals that are taken in externally.

Endogenous-are chemicals manufactured by our bodies.

Once the chemical enters the cell, a chemical reaction is created which then produces the physical response we feel relative to that emotion. As with all functions, the body wants to maintain perfect balance and over a short period of time the residue of that chemical reaction is removed and the physical reaction dissipates and goes away. Imagine how you would feel if that knot in your stomach and racing heart caused from a near accident lasted for days? It doesn't, only because of the body's innate ability to maintain balance.

While this process is maintained in perfect balance the majority of the time, it can become affected and damaged due to overstimulation. One of the key points to understand is that cells don't have a soul. They don't care if the chemicals are produced internally or externally or if they produce a positive or negative response in our bodies. They merely function according to their genetic coding.

If a cell receptor receives too much of one chemical over a sustained period of time, what happens is that it begins to malfunction. The normal chemical reaction produced and subsequent physical response begins to get out of balance. Over time the receptor is not able to create what should be the perfect physical response. Again, as the body is driven to maintain perfect balance, what happens is that the receptor does the only thing it can. It sends a signal to the brain, which sends you a subconscious message to do whatever is necessary to produce more of the chemical compound. As a result we end up repeating actions and behaviors unknowingly to satisfy the urge.

This leads to an actual chemical dependence. I often relate the story of my early days in radio. During late night weekend call in and request shows, invariably most weekends would produce a caller to my show who was sobbing and emotionally distraught. Fighting through the tears I would ask them what was wrong. A typical story would end with a line, *"He left me"* amid shudders and sobs. At the time I was just a radio announcer and would try and be nice and say, *"I'm sure this will all work out. Is there anything I could do for you"?* at which point they would reply, *"Can you play the saddest song ever"?* Every time I tell this story audiences break out into laughter. It seems absurd to any rationale thinking person that someone who is an emotional wreck would want a song that makes him or her feel more depressed and more distraught. The reason is simple. The craving this person was feeling to produce more of the chemical compound produced from depression happened completely on a subconscious level. The person is not even aware they are doing it. When we are sent these signals to repeat something that produces a negative result we are not consciously aware of it. If we were, we certainly would not do it intentionally.

We look at people who are addicted to chemicals and alcohol and say *"thank God that's not me"*. The truth is that it is you! The chemicals may come from a different source but we all have the capacity to become addicted to these chemical compounds produced in the brain just the same.

Like taking drugs or alcohol occasionally, one thought or one emotion does not create an addiction or lead to cravings. If however a behavior or emotion is repeated again and again it will. This is why more of the chemical is needed to produce a normal physical response which signals yet more of the behavior and drives us to invest in negative actions to produce it.

This has been proven out extensively in science with lab animals. During the experiments with primates, electrodes were hooked up to stimulate the production of the neuropeptides or chemical compounds produced by the hypothalamus. The animals were then trained to push a lever, which in turn would send a signal and produce more of the chemical.

What they discovered was that over a fairly short period of time the animals continued to push the lever again and again to produce more of the chemical. They ended up becoming so addicted to the chemicals produced in their own brain that they gave up food and water and sex and sleep and ultimately reached the point of exhaustion. Some of the animals almost died.

If you think about this you can see it in our everyday lives. We become so addicted to the production of these chemicals that we stay in bad relationships and continue to make negative choices. Again, the key point to this is that the reason we do not become aware of what we are doing is because it is all happening on a sub-conscious level.

It explains so much

- Destructive behavior
- The same situations over and over
- Inability to change
- Deep cravings for certain emotional responses.

Again, if we experience negative emotions occasionally, the cell receptors are not affected and they are able to maintain perfect balance. If however the same emotion is experienced again and again this is where the addictive behavior begins to come in. The cell receptors begin to send signals to the brain to repeat whatever is necessary to satisfy its need. The positive side to this process is that it is just as easy to become addicted to the chemicals produced from positive emotions as negative. Remember. Cells don't have a soul. They will become addicted to whatever chemical compounds they are over stimulated with.

To summarize the process of negative creating, below is the progression of events that lead to the creation of negative behavior.

- Negative input is taken in and is stored in our sub-conscious or memory
- This information is stored in a neuronet and as like information is input repetitively the neuronet grows in size and accessibility

- When the neuronet becomes larger we begin to access this information through cross-reference relative to current thought or action

- Over time this begins to impact our belief system and create doubt

- The doubt then begins to trigger activity that creates negative results in our lives

- These negative results by their nature create negative emotions

- The negative emotions then create the neuropetides relative to the emotion and they enter the cells

- If this process happens occasionally there is no impact on behavior

- Through the repetitive action of this emotion, the cell receptors begin to require more of the chemical to create the same feeling

- The cell receptors begin to send cravings to you on a sub-conscious level to repeat the same negative emotion or behavior in order to feed the addiction

- Ultimately, we end up repeating actions or thoughts that produce negative outcomes

This chemical addiction like the challenge of the voice in our head that leads to self-limiting behavior can be overcome. When the correct process is implemented over time, the actions and behaviors that were creating the negative emotions will slow and cease. When this happens the cell receptors will begin to recover and will stop sending signals on a sub-conscious level to repeat the behavior that you need to overcome. Once this process begins you will be able to input new information, create a new neuronet, produce positive results and create positive emotions, which will then lead ultimately to a change in behavior.

Here is the summary of the steps necessary to alter the process and change behavior.

- Negative actions are identified and stopped, which over time will cause the related neuronet to weaken, lessening their ability to be instantly accessed and impact current thought and action.
- Negative emotions will diminish which leads to the cell receptors becoming starved and over time the addiction to the chemical will lessen the craving that leads to the repetition of negative behavior
- New positive action and thought will begin to create new neuronets. Through repetition over time the neuronets will grow, rising higher in the filing system
- The access of the positive information in the new files will lead to the creating of increased positive results
- These positive results will create positive emotions
- Through repetitive action, the cell receptors will begin to crave this new chemical
- The cravings for the new chemicals will push you to repeat the positive behavior and emotions related to it on a sub-conscious level.

This is the process that is necessary for the creation of new positive behaviors. Here's where it all comes together. This new drive towards continued positive action through repeated focus on the desired intention then allows you to begin to manifest what you want in life, rather than what you don't want. Two dynamic exercises will be unveiled at the end of this chapter that will allow you to bring about the behavioral change you are deserving of.

In order to reverse the process that led to the self-limiting behavior that is responsible for creating our current reality there is a definite process that will enable you to do that. It begins with Passion. Defining your passion is that thing that moves you. It's the thought of an activity or purpose or desired result that creates a positive emotional response and begins the process of change. We have all felt great positive emotion in our lives before. Times like when we first fell in love or landed the big job or watched our child be born or bought our first home. That feeling of passion is something that to this day we can recall when the event is visualized again and played back in our mind.

Once you have been able to identify what your passion is, the ensuing process of change is greatly enhanced. Identifying your passion for what you want in life, who you want to become, where you want to go and what legacy you want to leave will become the driving force to begin the action required.

The Perpetual Motion of Success involves 3 key elements. The concept being that one element feeds the next, which feeds the next, and so on. As you continue to invest in these three elements, each will strengthen and produce increasingly positive results. Consider the process as being like the motion of a flywheel. As more pressure is applied on each element, pushing in the same direction the flywheel begins to turn and speeds up faster and faster producing greater and greater results.

- Passion drives you through a strong emotional connection to perform

- Visualization of your desired outcome will begin to engrain your goals into your sub-conscious mind

- Positive activity creates new positive emotions which in turn feed your cell receptors with the desired chemical that in turn drives more positive behavior

There are two exercises relative to the information covered in this chapter. The first will work to re-program the information in the files of your sub-conscious mind and the second will help you to alter the chemical link to emotions that are driving behavior. While the process is the same for everyone, the specifics of information and emotions will be entirely unique for each individual.

It is of great importance to understand that learning the information will do little more than entertain you. In order for real change to come about, it is essential that you commit to completing these exercises as they are described.

Re-Programming Exercise

The intention of this exercise is to begin to re-program the information currently stored in the files of the sub-conscious mind. We will be looking to alter just those files that are currently leading you astray. Again, every thought we have and every action we take is instantaneously cross-referenced with what we currently know or believe from the information stored in the files or neuronets. If the information says that *"I am no good at this or I can't have that or I am not worthy"*, no amount of effort will be able to overcome such crushing psychological adversity. *"If you think you can't, you won't"*.

Again, while the science is incredibly complicated the process is actually very simple. In order to accept what I am asking you to do all you need do is to ask the question of how the information that is in your sub-conscious mind got there is the first place? The answer is through the experiences of life and through repetitive intake. If we take in the wrong information over and over again we will end up being driven by the wrong information. If we take in the correct information we will be driven to do what is right which in turn will produce a positive result. Here is the core of this exercise. To cease accessing the wrong information and begin to input the correct information.

The concept of the exercises is to create a list of the behaviors you would like to change. To start out you are to create a list that is comprised of current goals and current doubts. The reason why the list must include current doubts is because some doubts are so strong that we would never even think to put them on the goals list. One example may be that an individual is terrified of public speaking. Given how they feel about this it is unlikely that this would make it onto the goals list. If however, becoming an effective public speaker is going to be a key to achieving their vision and life's goals, then this certainly must be on the list.

Once your list of goals and doubts is complete, the next step is to create your re-programming list. This list will provide the key information to be input into the sub-conscious mind that will allow you to overwrite the files. Here is the most important element of creating this list. It must be written in the present tense and framed as having already achieved it. Here is an example: If you wanted to lose weight and get in better shape, you are not to write, *"I am going to lose weight or I want to be in better shape"*. The reason being that the sub-conscious mind acknowledges the statement as something you don't have. What you must do is to write it out in the affirmative. *"I am at my target weight and I am in the best shape of my life"*.

The reason for this is that the sub-conscious mind can't differentiate between fact and fiction. Whatever information is input repetitively over a sustained period of time will cause the neuronet to grow, rising higher in the filing system, making it more readily accessed which will begin to form the belief. Ultimately this will cause the sub-conscious mind to believe it to be true. This belief is what will then direct your current and future actions.

Air travel is a perfect example of this psychological process. Hands down, it is statistically proven that air travel is the safest mode of transport on earth. I read a statistic on an app on my I-phone a while back that stated that more people are killed each year around the world by donkeys than by aircraft. Even given the overwhelming evidence that air travel is the safest, a great many people are terrified to fly. Here's why. Either through personal experience or self-talk they have input the information into their mind over and over again that the plane will crash and they will die. It's absolutely not true yet by repeating the message over and over again they then act *"as if"* they actually will die every time they fly. I have worked with clients on this re-programming exercise who began with a crushing fear of flying and over a period of 2-3 months were able to completely eradicate the fear.

Below you will find a list of suggestions of what a re-programming list may look like. These are suggestions only and your list should be created based upon your current goals and current doubts. The key to remember is to state this in the present tense as if you already have it.

- I love how great I feel because I eat well and exercise every day
- I found my calling and get to do it every day
- I am peaceful and calm in all situations
- I love to fly and enjoy all the places I get to visit
- I earn $_____ a year
- I attract success
- I am a great and powerful public speaker
- I continue to grow and learn everyday
- I am so confident knowing my destiny in life
- I am a great parent, spouse, and friend.

Once the list is completed, the next step is to begin to input the information into your sub-conscious mind. There is a good, better and best way of inputting the information.

- Good-read the list a minimum of 3 times per day
- Better-read the list out loud a minimum of 3 times per day
- Best-write the list out (written not typed) a minimum of 3 times per day

Now here is where the magic comes in. Start doing this and don't stop. After you have been doing this for a few weeks don't look around and ask, *"where is it"*. Don't give in to that liar in your head that questions everything you do. If you follow this simple protocol of starting it, doing it everyday and not stopping, more will change for you than you can imagine. This is not hocus-pocus. It's science. In essence what happens is that once the sub-conscious mind is convinced something is true (regardless of whether it is or not (example of the fear of flying) it will begin to direct you to invest in the action and activity that will make it true. This is how the brain works and you must know that you have the power to re-program anything you choose. The process will begin to produce substantive results within 2-3 months of beginning to do it every day.

Re-aligning our lives and creating a new belief system will not happen in a day. It will take time and it will take effort but the payoff is enormous. Living the life you choose as opposed to the one society has set out for you will provide incredible rewards. Consider the alternative of not doing it.

Positive Change Activity Exercise

The intention of this exercise is to alter behavior though the chemical process linking emotions to behavior. Through the detailed explanation in this chapter you should now be able to see the value of not only understanding the science but also understanding what is necessary to alter the process and to ultimately change the behaviors that are holding you back.

There are two aspects to this exercise that will work to alter the chemical balance from being controlled by what you don't want to becoming driven by what you do want. Again, one of the key points is to know that cells can't differentiate from one chemical compound to another. They don't have a soul. The process to become addicted to the chemical compounds or neuropetides is exactly the same for positive as it is for negative emotions. In order to move forward in any direction it is also critical to first address and negate the intake of more negative information. We have all heard the saying, *"Out with the old and in with the new"*. This philosophy has particular weight while going through this process of shifting your paradigm and moving from a negative to a positive position. There are two primary sources of negative information. These deal with the intake of information through the media as well and association.

1 *The news* is a primary source of negative imprinting on our psyche. Understanding that the beliefs we have formed have come from the intake of information, it stands to reason that taking in more of the negative will make the process of change more difficult. The news is something I understand very, very well. For twenty years I was the news and in the moment I truly believed we were doing God's work. We were taught and I believed that the information we were delivering to the public was essential. Having now been away from it for the past 9 years, looking back I can see it for what it truly is. The news is little more than a collection of train wrecks and tragedy with an occasional panda birth tossed in for good measure. If it truly were the *"news"* it would be the reporting of all of the events of the world but it does not. Ask yourself how learning of the next suicide bomber or murder or car crash is going to improve your life? The truth is it will not and never has. A key then as we go through this process is to turn it off. Eliminate the "news" from your day-to-day life. You will be amazed how much better you feel each day by not engaging in all of the pain and suffering of the world that does not have a connection or purpose in your day to day life.

2 *Association* is the second major factor that impacts negative conditioning on our sub-conscious. This association relates to everything from the books we read to the conversations we have and the people we spend our time with. All information that we take in will do one of two things. It will either enrich our lives or it will cloud it with more negatives. The brain is an incredible organ, capable of more than we can imagine but make no mistake. In order for it to function it must be fed. We can feed it hope and promise, victory and dreams, triumph and belief or we can

feed it sorrow and hatred, pessimism and failure, challenge and adversity. Think about this for a moment. How do you feel when you have a conversation with a friend or family member who is always upbeat and positive and who sees sunshine everywhere? Chances are you come away feeling uplifted and more positive than when you began. On the flipside, how to you feel after spending time with another who is negative or angry or depressed? Chances are you will come away feeling much of what they have given off. This applies to all information we choose to take in. What do you think will have a more positive affect on your mind? The story of triumph or the trashy novel of failure?

"If you want to improve your life, spend major time with major people, and minor time with minor people"

Creating Your Positive Change Activity List

In order to bring about the change in emotions from negative to positive, we must accept that it will come about through conscious effort. The structure of this exercise is to create a system that will stop negative emotions when they arise and re-direct your emotions towards positive. The chemicals created from consistent negative emotions as we learned would continue to create cravings on a sub-conscious level and push us to repeat more of the same. What you want to do here is to stop the behaviors that are not serving you and to create the ones that will.

This exercise is to create a list of positive activities that you know from past experience has the potential to create a positive emotion. This will in effect become a go to list in the moment when thoughts or events create negative emotions. We have all had past experience with things we have done that historically put us in a positive mood. From the music we listen to, the people we associate with, surroundings, activities and thoughts, all have personal historical relevance to positive outcomes and emotions.

Once the list is created, you are to carry it with you at all times, using it when necessary. The way to use this exercise is to become aware when negative emotions begin to take over. If you receive a troubling piece of news, something goes badly at work or you get into an argument, these all produce negative emotions. If you were to perhaps lose a big client it would be easy to allow it to trouble you and to stay in a negative state for an entire day or more. We now know what impact this will have on us on a chemical level and the potential risk we run for having it become self-perpetuating. When major issues arise, one of the challenges we also face is that if our trouble is shared with others they will likely support our staying in a negative state.

When you do find yourself overcome by a negative emotion, refer to your positive change activity list, pick one activity from it and do it. Initially some regard this process with doubt but here is what you need know. We are only capable of experiencing one emotion at a time. If you are having one emotion and you do something to create another, the new emotion will override the last and create a new psychological state. In most instances, change can come about quite quickly if you make the effort of re-direction. Once your mood and emotions have changed you will be able to return to your daily activities. The time expected to change your emotions will be no more than 15 minutes. The concept is to re-direct your emotion so that you may continue on with a productive day, rather

144

than allowing the emotion to sabotage hours or even days. Over time this continuous re-direction away from negative emotions will in fact begin to alter your chemically directed actions and the behaviors that control you.

This is the second stage of behavioral change. We can allow the negative emotion to continue to flood our bodies with the negative chemicals relative to the emotion or we can choose to change to the positive. Here are some suggestions of positive change activities. It is suggested that you create two separate lists. One that you will be able to utilize at work and the other during your private time. I guarantee that you will be fascinated at how quickly utilizing one activity from your list can produce a positive affect. Take the time to create the best list possible for future needs. The list below is meant to provide suggestions only. Take the time to create a list that is specific to your own experiences.

- o Calling existing satisfied clients
- o Lunch with co-worker
- o Phone call with friend or family member
- o Go for a walk in the park
- o Ask for assistance from a manager
- o Read a positive story from a book
- o Listen to uplifting music

Private time

- o Exercise
- o Go shopping
- o Look at family photos
- o Listen to favorite music
- o Read favorite uplifting book
- o Engage in a hobby
- o Call a friend or family member

Again, the key is that once your list is created to carry it with you every day and have it accessible when needed. Next we will move on to the process of growth and what is required both from a scientific and psychological aspect, but first, the story of two.

The Dream of Two Who Became One

Some would call it serendipity. Others call them omens. Still others would see it as old-fashioned true love, courage and hard work. This is not the story of one but of two who became one. Finding your own path in life is the challenge we all search for. When at that fork in the road of life's decision you meet another who is gazing down the same path the outcome can be extraordinary. This is the story of boy meets girl. Together they would go off to make their mark on the world.

Martin was the son of hard working immigrant parents. Farah grew up enduring the biting Winnipeg winters. They both attended Western University. Lived in the same apartment but never met. Their story some would say was written.

Martin was a year ahead of Farah at the University of Western Ontario. When the time came to sub-let his apartment, Farah's two friends came to check it out. Farah was not able to come that night and as a result the two didn't meet. They learned of this near meeting at a friends' cottage a year and a half later. At the time Farah had a boyfriend but for some reason the two kept bumping into each other. Her boyfriend moved away to Florida and Farah followed. As fate would have it, it didn't work out and six months later she came back home to Toronto. Shortly after Martin and Farah began dating. A year later they were engaged while Martin was finishing up articling for his law degree and Farah was working in a small ad agency. By the time they were married he had written his bar exam and became an associate lawyer at a large firm in the city.

One key moment in their lives came when circumstances offered up an opportunity to take some time to travel and reflect on life. Serendipity again playing its hand. There was a period of a couple of months between writing his bar exam and starting with the firm. The firm Farah was working for were cutting back her hours and they agreed to a sabbatical.

Their travels led them to exploring areas off the beaten track in Southeast Asia. At one point during the tip they ended up living with a hill tribe with no water or electricity. More than anything they noticed that these people were happy. During the trip a great deal of time was spent talking. The talk and what they were experiencing led to discussions of taking more control of their lives.

The return back to the path the world had chosen for them seemed void of passion and purpose. Martin's first day with the firm was at he beginning of February, joining the flock of blue suits and overcoats. He noticed so many that he was marching along with in this sea of responsibility looked miserable. When he returned home after his first day Farah asked, *"How was it"?* Martin replied. *"I don't think I can do this"*.

He wanted to leave that first day but felt the obligation of the world on his shoulders. The voice of his immigrant parents urging him to become all he could. The firm who helped out putting him through school added to the weight. Six months later he walked into the head partners office and informed him that this was not for him and he would be leaving. He was told, *"You are making the biggest mistake of your life"*. On his way out he wanted to say goodbye to a few other lawyers he had become close with. This same discussion with another lawyer sounded a bit envious and was supportive, *"You are doing the right thing. You are making a great decision"*.

Through the process of discovering their path, Farah had a discussion with her uncle who was a part time speaker and discovered that Farah was going into marketing. He asked if she could help market his services. That's how they stumbled on the idea of representing speakers. At the time Farah was working 20-30 hours a week and felt she could start a sideline business of providing marketing for speakers. At a speakers association meeting Farah met another speaker by the name of Jack Donohue who was also interested in marketing services for his speaking. He was instrumental in helping to guide them and lighting the fire.

During their research they noted that speakers wanted ultimately to book more engagements. At that point Martin said, *"doesn't it make sense if we booked them as well? You can do the marketing and I'll do the sales"*. And so their fledgling business was born. Their start up was run out of the spare room in their apartment and they reverted back to living like students to make it work. Friends would ask them to go for dinner but they had to decline because they couldn't afford it.

Martin, having never been involved in sales bought a book on making cold calls. His daily routine involved making 50-75 calls a day. Farah continued to work on marketing plans for speakers. The first six months of calling and marketing to meeting planners and potential speakers yielded only 6 bookings. Undaunted they continued on. The second half of the year saw them gain momentum and they booked more than five times what they had in the first six moths. They were encouraged. They far surpassed their goal in the first year and Farah quit her job. This was it. They had burned the ships and put everything they had into their new venture. What they began to notice was that even though they didn't have the money or lifestyle that their former jobs could provide they were happy. Happy was the key ingredient to their future success.

A second break came when two Toronto papers decided to write a story about their venture. The slant of one story was on couples working together. The other, that this new start up company was promoting the fact that there was great speaking talent in Canada.

Their story caught the eye of hockey's famous son, Paul Henderson who contacted them and met for a coffee. The year they began marked the 25th anniversary of his historic goal clinching the title for Team Canada. He was so impressed with their passion and ideas he decided to go with them. Having no previous experience in the speaking industry enabled them to offer creative solutions that had not been done before. They launched their website for $25 and were the first company to offer streaming video of their speakers. Throughout the development of the company they remained grounded and always looked to focus on long-term results and developing relationships.

Speakers' Spotlight is now the top speaking talent agency in the country. The company has grown from the spare room in their apartment to beautiful offices in downtown Toronto. They now boast a staff of 27, some of which have been there from the very beginning. Martin and Farah have remained true to their values and have worked to develop a culture by design and not default. Those who are on their team represent the same values that launched the company.

I asked what the most memorable moment during this journey has been. Along with the enormous impact of bringing the top speakers and minds to audiences around the world they recalled the story of Rubin Hurricane Carter who was falsely imprisoned for many years for a crime he did not commit. His dream he told them in a meeting, was to one-day meet Nelson Mandela. Two weeks later a request came through, booking Rubin to speak at World Reconciliation Day. The other speaker on the program was none other than Nelson Mandela. It was later discovered that it was his goal also to meet Rubin. Their dream now continues to foster the dreams of others every day.

The goodwill of their efforts now goes far beyond the speaking world and they have remained focused on giving back. A portion of every speaking engagement now goes to support KIVA.org. A micro lender assisting others from impoverished countries to make their dreams come true.

The dream of Farah and Martin has come a very long way since 1996. Last year they booked close to 2,000 engagements with some of the top speakers in the world. They told me they would likely never retire. To them this has never been work. It is a passion. I asked what advice they would give for another looking to jump off that cliff and follow their heart. They said, *"Go for it. What have you got to lose"?*

And so it is. The dream of two who became one. Speakers' Spotlight is the name given to their passion. To this day they continue to do what eludes so many others. They are living the life they designed.

5

Growth-Challenging the muscle

We are now moving on from altering behaviors to growth. The next element that will greatly assist you in achieving your goal of living the life you deserve is the understanding of growth both from a psychological and science based aspect. In the simplest terms here is the definition of growth. *"You are here, capable of doing this and you want to be there capable of doing that"*. As we discussed earlier, the process of achieving most anything in life follows this process. *"Set a goal, find out what is necessary to achieve it, begin to invest in the activity and don't stop until you have achieved it"*. This is a simple structure, however it is psychologically difficult to accomplish without a clear understanding of what it takes to go from here to there and to most importantly not stop along the way.

One of the great findings of science related to growth was the discovery of a substance in the brain and its function. Growth related to the increase in skill development and personal ability were long thought to be rooted in genetics, opportunity and even geography. What science learned was that growth; more specifically the rate of growth was linked to a process called deep learning. Deep learning is not ordinary practice or the passive intake of information. It is a highly targeted, error-focused process.

Every human action or thought, whether playing baseball, reaching a mathematical calculation or playing Bach is created by nerve fibers carrying a tiny electrical impulse throughout a series of brain cells or neurons. This electrical current in effect creates a mapping system to recall how a particular action or thought was completed. The route that the electrical signal travels along is called a neuro-pathway.

Now that we have covered how a thought or action occurs in the brain we are still on the edge of understanding how skill is improved. Again, it was long thought that genetics played the key role in this. What science discovered was that a seemingly innocuous substance in the brain is the key ingredient in the process of growth and skill development. This grey matter of the brain was thought to have little value. When the autopsy was performed on Albert Einstein it was discovered that he had approximately 30% more of this substance (myelin) that the average person. At the time it was discarded and dismissed. Now knowing it's importance and relevance to skill development we can look back and see why he had an abundance of it.

The function of myelin is to insulate the circuit or neuropathway. Its role is to wrap the circuits the same way rubber insulation wraps a copper wire, making the signal stronger by preventing the electrical impulse from dissipating. What results from a stronger signal is that it also travels faster. The process then is that the thicker the myelin becomes the better it insulates the circuit and the faster the signal travels. The faster a signal travels the better we become at the action or thought. In essence our skill relative to the insulation of the circuit is increased. The speed of the signal is in direct correlation to skill. From this we can see that:

Skill=Myelin

The process then, is that every time we repeat a thought or action the neuropathway or circuit is wrapped with myelin, which provides more insulation for the impulse or signal. The more the impulse or signal is insulated the faster it travels. The faster it travels the more skilled we become at that thought or action. How then can skill development be sped up? That question is at the root of the research into the process of myelination. The question then is how can we assist in the increased production of myelin and thereby speed up skill development?

The answer is described in the process of deep learning. The normal process of learning that we experience is the intake of information in a passive form. Reading this book is one example of passive learning. The information is being taken in; however the amount that sticks or becomes easily accessible through this process is limited. What science discovered was that through the process of activity/analysis (active learning) myelin production skyrocketed. In one experiment two groups of people were given the identical information to study. Group A studied for four one-hour periods. Group B were allowed to study for only one, one-hour period. Group B were then tested on the material 3 times. They were not given any of the answers but merely tested. Then both groups wrote an exam. The outcome was startling. Group B, who were only allowed to study a quarter of the time that Group A did scored 50% higher overall. This along with a number of other research studies proved the theory conclusively that active rather than passive learning was the key to the increase in skill development. What they discovered was that through this process, myelin production increased by up to ten times!

Deep practice then causes us to struggle in certain ways, operating on the edge of our ability. It's where we are forced to slow down, make errors and correct them. One of the researchers on the project said *"we tend to think our brains are recorders but that's wrong. They are living structures. The more we generate impulses, encountering and overcoming difficulties the more scaffolding we build, the more the circuit is wrapped. The more this happens the faster we learn"*.

A targeted effort can increase learning velocity tenfold. The process involves 3 simple facts

-1 Every human movement, thought or feeling is a precisely timed electrical signal travelling through a chain of neurons or brain cells.

-2 Myelin is the insulation that wraps these nerve fibers and increases signal strength, speed and accuracy.

-3 The more we fire a particular circuit the more myelin optimizes that circuit, and the stronger, faster and more fluent our movements and thoughts become.

Q: Why is targeted, mistake focused practice so effective?

A: Because the best way to build a good circuit is to fire it, attend to mistakes, then fire it again, over and over. Struggle is not an option. It is a biological requirement.

Q: Why are passion and persistence key ingredients?

A: Because wrapping myelin around a big circuit requires immense energy and time. If you don't love the process you are invested in, you won't repeat if often enough to become great at it.

The process of active learning involves working on at the edge of your ability then reaching, falling short, examining and reaching again. When considering how this applies in practical application it would follow the following parameters.

- o Pick a target
- o Reach for it
- o Evaluate the gap between the target and reach again
- o Return to step one

Myelination of a circuit when viewed under an electron microscope very much resembles the rings on a tree. Each wrapping or layer is a unique tracing of some past event. Ultimately the number of layers of myelin will be determined and impacted by encouragement, passion or incremental success. Each event produces another layer of myelin.

How this information relates to your process and how to utilize it in the best way you can is to ensure that as you move along your journey that you enlist the process of active learning. The best way to do this is to utilize the process of activity/analysis. For new information you are learning or skills you are developing, take the time to test yourself regularly. One very effective tool is to create a self-analysis form to review your own results and to test yourself. Again, the process of active learning increases myelin production by up to ten times. Myelin equals skill.

From skill development we now move on to the psychological aspects of growth. There are very specific steps and stages to the process of growth that ultimately impacts our results. The counter position is whether we continue with what is necessary to achieve our target at all. There is no question that you have all that you need at this exact moment in time to become and have anything you desire in life. The process of achieving your dream and life vision will require a consistent forward motion, likely through a number of different areas to arrive. Here is the absolute truth.

We have no idea what is inside of us until we challenge ourselves. If you cut open an acorn you would have no idea of the incredible potential it has to one day become a great oak tree. It is choice that creates the great disparity from one to another. One ends up on the streets homeless.

Another walks on the moon. Understanding this then, we can choose to reach our potential or succumb to self-limiting behavior.

"He who moves not forward, goes backward"

Johann Wolfgang von Goethe

The process of continuing to do what is necessary on a daily basis to move forward is almost entirely linked to belief. Belief is the voice in your head that says you can. Doubt is the voice that says you likely cannot. Walking the thin line between belief and doubt can be a tricky business and is the key element of growth. One of the greatest creators of doubt is time. Just the way we look at young people and say *"idle hands"* can lead to trouble, an idle mind will do the same. Here is the process. The further away we are from a target the longer the sub-conscious mind will have to offer up possible scenarios stored from past experience as to why what we are doing is not going to work. This process of negative thought begins to create doubt. Doubt leads to distraction. Over time we can become convinced that what we are doing is not working and stop. This is what in effect steals away our goals and dreams.

What must be done to overcome this is to take any goal and break it down into increments. What this does is greatly shortens the time between when a goal is identified and the time when it is achieved. The less time the stored negatives in the sub-conscious mind have to build a case for doubt the less chance there is to be convinced to stop. One other very, very important aspect to incremental goals is to ensure that the mind believes. By investing in the process of incremental growth, we begin to create the movie in our sub-conscious of what is possible. To create the belief that more is possible.

One of the great examples of this that I have witnessed personally was with a man by the name of Antonio. A number of years ago I ran a weight loss program on my radio show as an experiment. With the help of a certified nutritionist and trainer we put 10 people through a program of proper diet and exercise to measure the results. Antonio was one of the men who decided to take part. He had struggled with his weight for a most of his life. When he entered the program he weighed 330 pounds, had high blood pressure and type two diabetes. I remember on the first day when we all met at the gym. He was on a treadmill next to me, walking at the slowest pace for just 5 minutes. At the end he was breathing so heavy, dripping with sweat and was exhausted. Here is the magic. He came back. Within a week and a half he was up to 15 minutes on the treadmill. They started to work on his diet and began to teach him how to lift weights.

I remember having a discussion with him when his weight was getting down near 300 pounds. He said, *"You know Randy, for the first time in my life I believe I can make it to 275 pounds. You don't know what a difference that will make in my life"*. Success and growth leave clues. Incremental goals are essential. Here is what happened. As he began to approach 275 pounds his goal and belief changed and he said 250! The closer he got to 250 he said 225. As he closed in on 225 he said 200. When he began to approach 200 pounds he said, *"I'm going for it. I'm going to be in the best possible shape I can be"*. And he did. In the end he hit a final weight of 178 pounds with 7% body fat. This was and still is one of the greatest examples of the process of incremental growth I have ever witnessed.

Success and growth leave clues and ultimately *"Future belief is created through the motivation of personal incremental success through personal experience"*.

Throughout our lives we are taught that we are to learn from our defeats. There is no question that failure is one of the great teachers of life but becoming mired in what's wrong on a daily basis rather than what is right runs the risk of attracting into our lives more of what is not working. This is the core truth of the law of attraction. What we focus on expands. What we ignore dissipates. I was given a piece of philosophy years ago about this very topic and have never forgotten it. I was out for lunch with a mentor of mine, and the conversation ended up on golf. My mentor asked

"Do you golf"?

"Yes, I said. Just a few times a year".

"Do you watch golf on T.V."? he asked.

"Sure sometimes" I replied.

"Next time you do" he said. *"Watch them. Even the best. They are doing it all wrong"*.

"Really" I answered. *"Do you golf Bob"*?

"No, never a day in my life" he said.

He then went on to explain. He said *"Watch when one of the pro's hits a bad shot what they do. They will get back into the stance and swing through the same shot over and over again, throw the club to their caddy and then walk down the fairway in disgust. Watch the same golfer a hole or two later when he makes a great shot. He will toss the club to the caddy and then walk on down the fairway. What did he do wrong?"* he asked. I told him I didn't know.

"He's engraining the failure and letting go of the success" he said with a smile. He knew in an instant I could see he was right. It was fascinating to consider. But he was. Right that is. By stopping and swinging the club over and over again at the shot that went into the woods the golfer was engraining the failure into his sub-conscious mind. What he should have done was to get back into the stance over the shot that landed 3 feet from the cup and repeat, *"That was perfect. That was perfect. That was perfect".* It is so important to engrain our success rather than our failure. One final example of this is baseball. Baseball gets it. What is the most important number in baseball? The batting average right? Ty Cobb, the greatest batter in the history of the game batted .366. That means 634/1000 at bats he struck out. The focus should always be on how many we get right rather than how many we get wrong.

Remember, what we focus on expands.

The process of psychological growth (expanding our belief system) is almost exactly mirrored by physical growth. From a physiological stand point what happens when a muscle grows is this. When force is applied to the muscle (lifting or pushing) millions of micro-fibers in the muscle contract to perform the task. If what is being lifted or pushed is on the outer reaches of the muscle's ability, these micro-fibers tear. When this type of damage occurs the body rushes in to repair it. The result is that the micro-fibers they are made stronger and actually grow in size. This is what causes muscles to grow. The comparative to psychological growth is nearly identical.

Our current belief system is similar to a muscle. If our belief is caused to strain, we go beyond our current limit or comfort zone and there is damage to the micro-fibers of our belief. If the damage is not catastrophic it will be repaired and over time this, like our muscles, will become stronger and in effect settle in as our new belief or comfort zone. The analogy I use often in seminars is this. I ask the audience;

"Who here believes that I could lift two 50 pound dumbbells and do 3 sets of 10 bicep curls if I have not worked out in 10 years". Not one hand goes up . *"If I did try"* I continue on, *"What might happen"?* The response is *"You would likely hurt yourself".* *"So if I couldn't lift 50 pound weights, who here thinks I could lift 20's"?* Most hands go up believing I could. *"Alright then, if I lifted 20 pound weights today, could I then lift 50's tomorrow"?* The answer is of course not. I go on and say, *"So if I did 3 sets of 10 bicep curls for 2-3 weeks, 3-4 times a week could I then go to 25's"?* The answer is yes. Two more weeks to 30? Two more weeks to 35 and 40, then 45 and eventually 50? The answer is yes I could. Here is what we all learn from this then. I can lift 50 pounds. Just not today. Psychological growth follows the exact same principles.

As with physical growth we can't expect our psychological belief to be placed under an incredible burden and have it survive. This is why incremental growth is so critical to the process of achieving the goals we set. The incremental goal, just like the increments of weight we lift must match our current belief. If our current comfort zone is linked to the belief that we can earn $60,000. a year, there is little chance we can change our belief in one day to $500,000. The incremental goal then may be to grow our income to perhaps $70,000. If your own personal belief is that, *"yes, I believe I could accomplish that"* then it will happen. Once the new comfort zone begins to establish you could challenge it again and say, *"I believe it would be possible to earn $80,000. a year".* Just as we saw with the story of Antonio who went from 330 to178 pounds, it was the incremental targets along the way that allowed for the ultimate prize of such incredible health. If Antonio had been asked when he began at 330 pounds if he thought he could reach 178 he would have never believed it and would have succumbed to doubt long before he reached the target. Here is what all of this means then. If your current incremental goal does not match your belief, success is all but impossible.

One final example of the importance and power of incremental growth is karate. My youngest son is taking karate and after seeing the structure I was amazed by how intelligent the system is. If you ask anyone what the goal is in karate they will tell you that it is to get your black belt. The reality is that in order to achieve black belt status you would have to study for between 6-8 years, attending classes 3-4 times per week. Understanding how psychologically challenging this task is, karate decided that they needed their students to have something to focus on, (an incremental goal) along the way.

As such they created a number of other belts of various colors that students earn on their way to the black belt. Here is the question, *"Have you ever heard or seen someone going around bragging to the world they were a green belt or a yellow belt or a blue belt"?* The answer is no, yet they all exist for one purpose only. To create an incremental goal to keep students engaged in the process. For my son this philosophy is taken even one step further. The length of time to go from his white to yellow belt is likely about 9 months. Knowing this and understanding that to a child this feels like an eternity, what his karate school does is that when they learn a segment of the first kata they are given a piece of black tape on their belt. When they have 6 pieces of black tape they are awarded their next belt. Pure genius! By doing this, the focus goes from the only thing that really matters which is the black belt, to the yellow belt and then to the next piece of black tape. In order to secure your ultimate goal of living the life you deserve, you will also have to follow this process of incremental growth.

"The commitment to grow just an inch a day will provide you with a view of the world from a height of over thirty feet in just one year"

The following is a simple structure that will allow you to implement the process of incremental growth.

Exercise

Every goal that we set out to achieve has a beginning, end and a few or a great many parts in between. The increments necessary to achieving any goal have structured action steps but more importantly they carry with them the psychological necessity of belief. It is the psychological commitment linked to belief that we must pay particular attention to. Using the analogy of lifting weights, as you move forward towards your goal ask yourself this question.

Main Goal:

My goal is to _____

My incremental goal over_____this period of time, I believe I can

accomplish_____this.

Again, the key is that *your own belief* must match the incremental element of the goal. Once you have achieved the incremental element, re-evaluate the next step and next increment. Again it must match your own belief. This simple yet absolutely necessary process will allow you to continue doing what is necessary to arrive at your destination. Next we will delve into the development of one of the most important skills in life for anyone; focus. Before that, the story of the magic man.

The Magic man

"His life is magic, but there's no illusion"

Tears welled up in his eyes recounting the earlier days of his journey. The eyes they say are windows to the soul. You could see that he was right back there. Reliving the memories as if they were yesterday. The early days of his life; up until the age of 13 he told me was a time when he could not recall one happy day. Not one. Some who experience such darkness succumb and never see their potential. Others crave light so bad they jettison far beyond where most would end up.

He was born in 1970, the year of the Kent State shootings and the October crisis. There were no notable events in Dan's life with the exception of the abuse and beatings at the hands of his mother's long list of alcoholic boyfriends and sometimes husbands. His real father made his escape for the left coast when Dan was just 4 and never returned. He recalled the plan his mother drilled into them to deal with the many men who paraded through his life. He was told to always have a pillowcase of clothes packed at the ready if they needed to escape in the middle of the night. Many times they did. One of the men in his mother's life held the family hostage. It ended in a shoot out with police. His mom moved from restaurant to restaurant working as a waitress. The constant was that he never knew what was for dinner until he checked the take out containers.

When Dan was 13, in the summer between grade 8 and 9, he came home one day and the entire apartment was empty except for his clothes and a few bits of furniture. There was a note from his mom saying that she would explain later. She never did. The only way he could avoid being taken by the Children's Aid Society was to create the illusion he was still living with his mom so he got a job to pay the rent. The job he landed was at a local pig farm shoveling manure 7 hours a day after school. 2 years later while riding his bike to work he could smell the smoke. The barns had burned down and along with it went his job, only income and ultimately a place to live. After losing the apartment he ended up living and sleeping where he could. Discovering his plight, one of his teachers helped him get a job cleaning the cafeteria at school. It provided the opportunity to take the leftovers to eat. His other school job of washing the football team uniforms allowed him a place to do his own laundry.

When he was 14 he landed a job at a local cabinet making business. The man who entered his life was the owner Glenn Steele. One day when the labor board was there inspecting they asked *"Who is the boy working out in the shop"*? Glenn replied, knowing because of his age that it was illegal, *"He's my son"*. From that day on Dan called him dad. For the next 22 years until he passed away that was who he was. The image of the man who became his dad is always evident. Dan tattooed his portrait on his chest. A tribute to an incredible man who reached out and made a difference in the life of a boy who was invisible to the world.

Through all of the challenges growing up he was still able to complete high school. He opened a fledgling tattoo parlor with his brother at age

19. That venture would lead to a chain of 4 stores and a mobile studio. *"At one point"* he said, *"We were making $1,000. a day"*. Deep down Dan was driven to be an entertainer. After several tries and without any experience he was able to convince the local radio station that he could produce the morning show. I know how hard he tried to get the job because it was my show. I was the one who hired Dan. I was also the one who let him turn on the microphone, become a part of the show and flourish as an entertainer. He was not just the guy who pushed the buttons. He became a huge part of the show and would eventually move on to have his own.

The tattoo shops continued to grow to the point where it allowed Dan and his family to take a year off to travel and shop. Something he still finds fascinating. When they returned a sleep disorder led him to seek out help from a hypnotist. The impact it had on his life left him so inspired that he studied and became a certified hypnotist himself. Always the entertainer Dan also began to study magic and to develop tricks of his own. It was on the steps of a local music store that he and a friend came up with the name Danny Zzzz . His first show was at the Canadian Auto Workers hall for $5. a ticket.

It was the decision to combine magic with hypnosis that saw his new career take off 2 years later. Dan was signed on 5 years ago to perform at Casino Niagara. To date he has performed more than 1,400 shows and was recently selected as the only Canadian finalist in an international magic competition with Juri Geller and Chris Angel. Last year he presented his story and show to the TV program Dragons Den and received support from all 5 judges. Some of his magic highlights include a blindfolded car ride as the driver and a recent stunt, hanging suspended from a helicopter upside down while escaping from a straight jacket. If you want to see some of his magic you can visit him on YouTube at dannyzzzz1. His act and talents are now allowing his passion and talent to be seen all over the world. There is plenty of magic left in him and more than enough to smile about today. A smile that eluded the first 13 years of his life. It is no illusion that he is one of those, who after being handed more than his share of obstacles chose his own path and now is living the life he designed.

6

Focus

One of the great tools at our disposal to achieve more and to have what we are deserving of is a skill we have always had. It is a skill that will serve you greatly in your quest to follow your heart and make your dream come true. That is your ability to focus or what I refer to in seminars and coaching programs as Current Moment Consciousness.

Studies show that the average person is "here" somewhere between 1-15% of the day. To clarify the point, being *"here"* is in reference to being focused and engaged on this exact moment in time. Not being *"here"* is in reference to the time spent lost in thought thinking about our client or our bills or the economy or challenges or the BBQ on the weekend. It is a fact that the brain can only process one thought at a time. Given that, it is a fact we can't be "here" and be "there" at the same time. As adults the amount of time we spend "there" is enormous.

The most often stated intention for developing focus is to increase productivity. There is no question that it will and it does. When trying to improve focus what we are looking to do is to replace the distractive voice in our mind with productive, task-oriented thought. There is no question that improving our ability to focus will have an untold impact on productivity, however and perhaps more importantly, the net gain of improving focus is that it also greatly impacts our quality of life. Here is the end game on a personal level. When you are at the table with your family, you get to be at the table. When you are playing with your kids on the floor, you get to be on the floor. When you are with a client you get to be with the client. This is truly one of the most powerful skills anyone can learn.

The true definition of developing the skill to focus goes far beyond the ability to increase productivity. Here is the definition:

"To be free of the psychological need of the past for your identity and the future for your fulfillment"

What this means is that both the past and future are illusions and steal away enormous amounts of time to be here. Not being able to shut off that voice in our head is a terrible affliction. The reason why we don't realize this is because almost everyone is suffering from it. It is one of those accepted norms of society that says *"if enough of us are suffering then the suffering must be normal"*. You can no doubt see the error of this philosophy.

One of the major reasons why the voice in our head is so powerful is because it is ego driven. To our ego, only the past and future are considered important. The voice in our head keeps the past alive for our identity and it projects our thoughts constantly into the future to ensure its survival and to seek fulfillment. We have brief moments of current focus directed by our ego when we are receiving an immediate reward through such actions as winning an award, having sex, closing a sale or picking up a new car.

Otherwise our ego leads us to believe that *"Everything will be fine when I have this or achieve that or become something that I am not now"*. We are constantly tricked into accepting that *"I'll be happy when"*. We are misled into believing the answer always lies in tomorrow. Here is the definitive question as to the importance of constantly looking to the future. *"Was today not one of those tomorrows we held out so much hope for?"*

I realized the incredible importance of the moment one day walking by the island in our kitchen. Sitting on the corner were a stack of photographs that had just been picked up from the photo shop. I stood there for a few minutes looking at them reliving the moments and the memories. I thought of a conversation most of us have about their importance. *"If there was a fire in your home and you got the people and pets out, what one other thing would you want to rescue that you couldn't replace"?* Most will say *"My pictures"*. Given that, we can then see just how important they are.

I then began to do the math and thought that if I had 5,000 pictures (which would be quite a few) how much time would they represent? If we allowed for one second for each to be taken that would equal a grand total of only 83 minutes of life! Lets put this into context. The 3rd most reported thing of importance we have in life is our pictures and they represent just 83 minutes of our lives. Are there times in life when a memory was created where you did not have a camera? The answer is of course. We can all recall the great experiences in life. The moment our children were born, the great vacation or dinner or memory. Now consider this. It is not possible to experience a moment if we are *"there"* lost in thought. Given that, imagine just how much of our lives slip by that don't create mental photographs or memories? This is something completely within your power. This is a skill you can have great dominion over which will serve you now and for the rest of your life.

There are two very clear symptoms of not living in the moment. They are stress and fear. Here is what stress and fear say. *"I'm here and I want to be there."* The reality of life however is that until we get *there* you don't get to know. Your mind convinces you that the reason you want to be there is so you can know if what you imagined would come true or if a problem you perceived was avoided. While stress and fear most often comes from the unknown future, it can also come from thinking of the past. We focus on the problems we encountered or the belief that it was so much better then. We romantically recall the past and wonder why it is not as good now as it was then.

An example of this would be that how you would react and what would happen if you were driving to work on a Monday morning and felt the transmission slip. Immediately you would worry about how much it's going to cost to fix and where you will get the money. You call your mechanic and are told that he is booked up until Friday. *"Just drive easy"* you are told *"and check the fluid and you should be fine"*. After hanging up you go back to worrying. You worry all day Monday, Tuesday, Wednesday and Thursday. Then Friday finally arrives and you take it to the mechanic.

He puts it up on the hoist, drops the pan, does something then lowers the car down. He walks out, looks at you and says, *"Listen, the bands were just a bit loose. I've tightened them up. You are good to go. No charge".* You stare at him in disbelief and think to yourself, *"What do you mean no charge? You owe me a bill. After all the worry I put into this all week long you owe me a bill".*

Think about it. How many times do we do this? How many times do we go down that rabbit hole of stress and worry and what we imagine almost never comes to fruition. If you are like most, this is nearly always the outcome. Imagine then just how much life is wasted with nothing to show for it? This is time we will never get back. Time that once stolen away can never be put into the column of achievement. Using the example of the transmission, if there had been a bill of $1,000., the time wasted during the week could have been used to actually earn some of the money to pay the bill but instead it would have been squandered.

The reason fear is the great occupier of the mind is because we feel we have no control over it. Remember that fear is not real, it's imagined. The one thing that is real is the emotion. There is no question that when we internalize a fear the emotion will be experienced even on a physical level. Fear makes our perceived problems seem bigger than life. Fear comes to us in the form of unease, anxiety, nervousness, tension, dread and phobias.

Coming to terms with fear lies in the definition itself. Fear: *"A negative emotion related to something that might happen, not something that is happening."* Most have heard of the acronym. F.E.A.R –*False evidence appearing real.* By making the commitment to stay in the moment fear will have no place to live and grow. A very common fear people have is the fear of flying. Books are written on this. Experts work tirelessly to help those gripped by it to overcome it. Consider the number of people in the world who are afraid to fly even though it is statistically proven that flying is the safest form of travel in the world. The amount of time and energy wasted with no negative outcome is staggering and this is just one fear. The time wasted on this or any fear will never be recovered.

The question at this point to ask yourself is this. *"Is it possible for someone who is constantly stressed out and living with fear to overcome this and begin to live in the moment"?* The answer is every time. One of the great stories of an incredible turn around involved a gentleman in the late 1800's who was a medical student was attending Montreal General Hospital. At the time he was worried about everything. He was worried about his grades and he was failing. He was worried and stressed out about how to start a practice. Whether he would find a wife. The state of the economy. Everything. Then one day in the library at the hospital he picked up a book that changed his life. The book was written by one of the great writers of the day, Thomas Carlisle. There was a passage of 21 words that changed his life. The passage read;

"It is not our goal to see what lies dimly in the distance but to do what clearly lies at hand."

Those words spoke to him and made him realize the error of his ways. He began to see the enormous amount of time he was spending on stress and fear and realized that it was actually responsible for his accomplishing so little.

From that day on he began to realize that overcoming stress and fear and learning to live in the moment was the most important skill he could master. Great change does not come in a day or week. Great change comes from the consistent application of reasonable effort day after day. He began to work on this and in his mind created what he referred to as Day-tight compartments where he called the past the dead yesterdays and the future the unborn tomorrows and acknowledged this was the only moment in time he could produce anything.

As his skill of becoming more focused improved so did his life. His marks began to improve to the point where he was able to turn a failing grade around to graduating from medical school. He went on to become one of the founders of John's Hopkins Medical Center. He became Regis Professor at Oxford University and was knighted by the King of England. When he died it took 2 volumes and 1481 pages to tell his life story. His name was Sir William Osler. During an interview late in life, he told the interviewer that if you asked his friends or family or colleagues they would tell you that he was of the most ordinary mind. He said, *"All those years ago I learned that this was the only moment I could create anything and it was as a result of that, that allowed me to create the body of work I did over a lifetime"*. What an amazing story and a lesson to us all. I have thought many, many times over the years about his story. In my mind I pictured myself standing beside him in the library that day while he pulled out the book and read the passage. I thought of how his life would have turned out if he paid the words no heed. If he had not improved his ability to focus, what would we call him today? "Billy the dockworker"? This would have more than likely happened had he not mastered this skill. The part of this story that fascinates me more than anything is that Billy the dockworker and Sir William Osler was the same guy. Understand that improving your ability to focus is one of the most important skills you can master. It will allow you to become the person you are capable of being rather than the person that you currently are.

It is important when learning any new information or concept to understand how the brain works. The brain sees in pictures and not in how we view communication. If you are asked to see an elephant you don't see the letters, E.L.E.P.H.A.N.T, you see a big grey floppy eared creature. With this in mind I want to discuss three forms of thought and the metaphor that will allow you to visualize them. Consider this. In this scenario you have the choice of driving 3 vehicles to your destination. The vehicle that you allow your mind to occupy is what will determine the outcome and success of your day.

The first vehicle you may choose is that of the past. This vehicle is a rusted out old model T up on blocks without an engine. This vehicle is incapable of moving. It is yesterday's vehicle and incapable of going anywhere. The second is the concept car of the future. Again, it is impossible go anywhere in it because it is just a shell and has no engine. You can look at it, admire it, picture yourself sitting in it but it has no engine or moving parts, as it is just a concept. The result is that forward motion is impossible.

The third car is a car of today. Picture the car you currently drive. This is the only vehicle of the three that has the ability to travel. Now lets look at a mathematical equation.

"If you spent one hour in the antique car on the highway how far would you travel?" The answer is not an inch.

"If you spent one hour in the car of the future on the highway how far would you travel?" The answer is not an inch.

"If you spent one hour in your car on the highway how far would you travel"? The answer is 100km or 60 miles.

The next calculation to consider is this.

During an 8-hour day if you travelled on the highway based upon the parameters below, how far would you travel in total?

3 hours in antique car	0 km
2 hours in car of the future	0 km
3 hours in your car	300 km
Total travelled	300 km

Now the next day if you decided to spend one less hour in the antique car and one less hour in the car of the future and spent that time driving your car on the highway travelling at the speed limit, how much further would you travel?

The answer is 200 km further or 120 additional miles. Over the course of a year by spending just 1 less hour in each of the antique and future cars you would travel nearly twice the distance around the earth. Over a 30-year period you would travel an ADDITIONAL 1.3 million more miles! This calculation has an exact mathematical correlation to thought and what we can accomplish or conversely what we loose. The question the is, *"If you worked to improve our ability to focus on this moment in time, what could you do with an additional 2 hours of total focus each day"*? The answer is more than you could imagine.

Hopefully now you see the value to improve this skill for yourself. Again, as with any change in life, understanding the information is key, but investing in the activity that will actually bring it to fruition is where the magic lies. Here is what you must know and accept about improving your ability to focus. It takes time. It happens slowly. You won't actually notice the improvement from one day or even one week to the next. If you do invest in the process laid out below, your ability to focus over a period of 2-3 months will improve dramatically. Adopt this for a lifetime and experience a new life.

We start with the asking of two questions that will begin the process of improving your ability to focus. These questions will address the types of thought we have and the quantity. Our brain is like the C.P.U. (central processing unit) of a computer. It is capable of producing a finite number of thoughts in one day. What we also need to understand is that the brain is only capable of processing one thought at a time. Again, our objective is to focus thought where it can have the greatest impact, which is here in this exact moment in time.

The first question is in relation to thought that is grounded in stress and fear and can in no way affect an outcome. This type of thought is generally about something we are waiting for in the future or worried about from the past. The example of the car transmission relates to this type of thought. We can't know the outcome until the car is taken in to the mechanic. As such no amount of thought about the transmission can alter the outcome. When we do have this type of thought, you are to stop and ask this question:

"Is there a problem in this exact moment?"

Generally, our problems are linked only to our perceptions of what *may* happen. Ask yourself this question at this exact moment in time. *"Do you have a problem in this EXACT moment"?* The answer with great certainty the absolute majority of the time is no. Here is what you are to do then. Whenever you feel stressed and are having a thought that you can have absolutely no control over the outcome, simply stop and ask the question. The reason for this is that over time you will begin to alter the subconscious mind to know the truth which is *"I don't have problems, I perceive I have problems".* What will begin to happen is that every time you check in with yourself to see if you have problems you will be made to understand that you don't. The continuation of this process will begin to reduce the amount of this type of thought as it will be understood to be of no value.

The next question is this.

"Do you carry inside of you the burden of 100 things that need to be done?"

Almost everyone does. If we have 100 things on our mind and we think about each one over and over, imagine how much time is taken up by this process. The first step is to understand why? Why do you carry around the list of all those things that need to be done? The dry cleaning that needs to be picked up. The bathroom that needs to be painted. The client to call. The check book to balance. The new shoes to buy. The list goes on and on. So the question then again is, *"Why do we keep repeating in our head over and over again to pick up the dry cleaning or to call the client"?*

The simple answer is that we don't want to forget. Think of the burden of the 100 things that need to be done in this way. On the inside of your skull are a hundred sticky notes and written on them are each of the things that needs to be done. If you don't repeat what's on the note often enough the adhesive will let go, it will slip off and you will swallow it and you will forget. The only way for it to stay there is to repeat it over and over again. Is this a productive use of thought? Of course not. The answer then is to do this. Whenever you have a thought that requires action, take it out of your head and put it somewhere. It could be a notepad or a voice recorder. I use the recorder on my phone because it takes just a few seconds and I'm not always looking for a pen. When something comes to mind that I need to take care of I simply leave myself an audio note. At the end of the day I listen back to what I recorded, take the information and enter it into my calendar.

- o Dry cleaning: Wednesday at noon.
- o Call the client: Friday at 10
- o Paint the bathroom: Saturday morning 9am

Once the thought has been put into my recorder I can then let it go and will no longer be forced to repeat it. The cumulative affect of the amount of thought time saved from this simple exercise is enormous. Again, when you have a thought that requires action, take it out of your head and put it somewhere.

Exercise

The following exercise will provide a structure to improve your ability to focus steadily over time. Gaining dominion over your mind is one of the great skills of life.

-1 Make the commitment that *"you will only allow your mind to focus on the thought that can produce results at this moment"*. This is a statement that should be added to your re-programming list. The repetitive input of this information over time will program the sub-conscious mind to adopt this as a firm belief. This sub-conscious belief will then direct you to carry out what the sub-conscious mind now believes.

-2 The next part of this exercise of training the mind to be more focused is to work on becoming the observer. For one week you are to begin the process on small tasks when things are going well and free of stress. The objective is to try and give total focus on average daily activities like walking up stairs, eating a meal or showering in the morning. Clear you mind and become completely focused on the activity. When a thought comes in push it out. While putting focus on these errant thoughts you will begin to actually hear what is going on inside of your brain. It can be somewhat alarming at times and amusing as well. *"I can't believe I was thinking about that. What a total waste of time"* is a common response while doing this. Carry this exercise out as often as possible for a one-week period before moving on.

-3 The next phase of increasing our ability to focus is following the one-week period of practicing on small tasks, you are going to begin to build on the process. This skill is like a muscle and it must have pressure put on it to grow slowly and incrementally over a period of time. In this phase you will begin to apply conscious focus for a short period of time. Each day choose one activity that you have planned and commit to focusing as much as you possibly can for a period of 15 minutes. As you are working to apply as much focus as you can, when a thought comes in push it out, a thought comes in push it out, and so on. Commit to this every day for the first week and then expand the time by 5 minutes each week. This will begin the process of building the muscle to allow you to be focused on the moment for longer periods of time.

One final point is that when executing the task at hand, don't concern yourself with the fruits of the action. The purpose of the exercise is to simply train your mind to focus on the moment again and again. Often times when working on improving the ability to focus people will attempt to measure whether or not the improved focus is producing a better than average result. Again, this simple action of judgment will take you out of the moment and break your focus. Coming up you will begin to formulate the structure and daily discipline over actions and activities, but first the story of the son of a preacher man.

"We all have the ability to become much more than our mind currently allows us to believe"

The Son of a Preacher Man

Y ou'd never know from a first meeting what had gone on in his life or what his personal journey had entailed. Appearances can be deceiving. A slim build, a pale complexion, a quiet demeanor and a shy personality would provide no clues to what had come before in the life of this young man.

He was born in the late '70s to parents still flirting with their teenage years; his father was 22, his mother just 19. Though their years were few, their maturity was well beyond those years and his arrival was not only expected but very much wanted. The early years of his life were typical middle class, with a wonderful home, a great school, little league and many friends.

His first struggle in life came at the age of 7 when his parents faced the challenge of many young couples that try to make a life too early. Their divorce was devastating for him and proved to be his first taste of the obstacles that life can throw your way. The ensuing years changed his world into one of growing up in a single-parent home while spending time with his father on weekends.

Personal strength comes in many forms, and at age 15, while dealing with the struggles in his life, he made the decision to move away from everything he'd ever known to start his life over living with his father two hours away. The courage that this decision took was incredible. By deciding to get his life on track, he walked away from everything familiar and everything that provided grounding - his mother, the only home he'd ever known, schoolmates he'd known since junior kindergarten, minor sports and more.

The first few months after his move were very difficult. His shyness made it hard to make new friends and to fit into a new school and community. He was also faced with the new challenge of fitting into a blended family with two siblings from a mother he didn't share. Because of his shyness, his father drove him to school and picked him up for lunch almost every day so he wouldn't have to sit alone to eat. For quite some time, it appeared that perhaps the move had been a mistake and that it was going to be too hard for him to start his life over from scratch.

Over time, his shyness ebbed and he was able to make friends. The one constant in his life was his father, who had always encouraged him to follow his dreams and to do with his life what he truly loved. As the months turned into years, he continued having conversations with his father about life and what direction he'd like to take. There were glimmers of hope that he'd found something he was passionate about, but those hopes would soon fade.

Later in his teen years, the boy developed an interest in music. Not just any music. Though he'd grown up in predominantly white neighborhoods, he became drawn to all forms of black music and the culture that surrounded it. A voice inside told him that this was what moved him. This was what created passion in his heart.

While his record collection grew and the posters fanned out over the walls of his room, his father took note and encouraged his son to follow his passion. While still in high school, he volunteered at a local radio station, sensing that this would give him an opportunity to be close to the music. At the same time, he showed his strength by holding down as many as three part-time jobs to help to buy his clothes, music and his first car.

Over time, the volunteering paid off and he was hired to work part time in the promotions and music department. Two more jobs would come up at radio stations during his school years, pushing him still closer to his true love. During his second year of university, he was offered a job as an assistant music director for little more than minimum wage an hour's drive from his home. The job was full-time and provided a great challenge: He wouldn't be able to accept the job and continue his schooling. After many phone calls, many discussions and soul-searching with his father, the decision was made to leave school and take the job. His father had been telling him for years to do what he loved, and it appeared that this was it.

That first job was by no means an open door to his dreams. The format of the station was very different from the music he loved, and the low pay, long commute and financial challenge still required him to hold down part-time jobs to make ends meet. But he was undaunted.

Over the next three years, he took jobs at competing radio stations and worked tirelessly at learning the craft of music programming. His hard work and passion for his love paid off: His next posting would make his commute an hour longer but land him face to face with his ultimate dream. Today that station is the largest and most successful black urban radio station in the country and was recently named radio station of the year for all of Canada.

Should you find yourself in Toronto and have a chance to listen to FLOW 93.5, you'll hear the music programmed by that shy, unassuming white guy who had a dream years ago that society gave him little hope for achieving. Society forgot to take into account his passion. Passion can overcome all.

This story is a continuation, really. It's the story of the young boy you read about earlier who sat in his walker all those years ago and tried to pick up the apple. The story is about my son Justin. I believe it's important to provide examples of average, everyday people who have been able to do extraordinary things with their lives. If the only stories we read are of successful people who have achieved great celebrity status, the inclination is to conclude that "I" could never be one of "them." Again, success is not to be defined by anyone other than the person who feels the passion. Success is quite simply the ability to design your own life and pull it off. There's no question that he pulled it off. Justin was faced with more than his share of "cant's" but pushed on. He's the epitome of success and is an incredible example of what's possible when you dream. I know he's one of the lucky ones. I asked and yes, every week he does "*Look forward to Mondays*".

7

The Self-Directed Solution

"The definition of failure is a few errors in judgment each day. The definition of success is a few disciplines repeated each day"-**Jim Rohn**

Following our life's passion and creating our own journey often times leads us along a singular path of a self-directed nature. While not all people leading an authentic life strike out on their own as an entrepreneur, a majority will find themselves in this position. Regardless of whether you end up self-employed or if you find your path within an organization, this process will all apply to both. Taking charge of our lives is a philosophical first step. Creating the structure and discipline to be productive and effective is the next ingredient in the caldron of success. Without realizing it most have adopted the philosophy to "get through the day". This process is designed to help you to get "from the day". After all, our time here is not unlimited. We have a finite number of days and they will bring us to life's end. It's what we do with the today's and the tomorrows and the days after that, that will determine where we end up. *"Live today, because there will never be another today"*. The actual difference between those who struggle and those who excel if far less than you may think.

It's easy to stand back and believe that those who are achieving far more than the average person are workaholics or a golden spooners or just "lucky". What you are likely to find is they are not. They are simply investing in a reasonable amount of the right activities each and every day and not leaving life to chance. The true difference between success and failure is this. Success is the repetition of a few disciplines daily. Failure is the repetition of a few errors in judgment repeated daily. There is no big bang theory. I did not succeed today and I will not fail today. (Unless Oprah calls) I joke with audiences all the time and tell them that this is true unless Oprah calls. If Oprah calls you just buy the cottage. But if Oprah doesn't call, here's what we have to do. To invest in a reasonable number of disciplines daily. Therein lies the magic and we all have the ability to do that. This is the story of the tortoise and the hair. The finish line to success is not a wind sprint. It's a steady journey of the implementation of a reasonable number of disciplines repeated daily. No more and no less.

As we are about to discuss the structure and philosophy of what has become referred to by clients over the years as 'the boss/employee relationship" I want you to know this process has been in place and used by all of my professional coaching clients with astounding success. It was interesting many years ago when I created this that I felt a sense of unease wondering if it would be perceived as too simplistic and obvious.

The intention of implementing this process is to improve productivity and income, reduce stress and create a daily sense of purpose and accomplishment. As a self-employed or self-directed individual here is the greatest challenge. When you sit down at your desk each day what do you have to do? While the actions and activities may vary from person to person, the reality for us all is the same. "Everything!!" As a self-employed or self directed person you have to do everything and it feels overwhelming and distracting and daunting. Trying to balance business growth and marketing with client service and training, hiring and firing, picking up the dry cleaning and making it to soccer practice on time feels like an endless conveyer belt of impossibility. The reality is that those who master this process are the ones who are propelled forward and achieve success. Those who don't remain mired in frustration wondering why they can't make it happen.

My greatest asset in helping clients to implement this new process and philosophy is that most everyone have experienced this structure at some point in the past. For us all there was a time when we had a boss and we worked as an employee for either an hourly wage or salary. While I realize that I am stating the obvious, here is the structure. The employee agrees to provide a stated number of hours of service in exchange for a salary or hourly wage. The tasks that are to be completed during these hours are delegated by the management or boss of the individual. In effect, the employee is given a list of tasks each day. There is a firm understanding that the employee is to finish everything on the list. If they do, they remain employed and are paid a salary.

If the employee is diligent, finishes everything on the list each and every day of the year and works above and beyond what is asked of them, the company may choose to reward them with a bonus. For most an anticipated bonus may be cost of living. An extremely generous bonus would be 10%. On a salary of $100,000. per year the annual bonus would amount to $10,000. before taxes.

It is widely agreed to by most that it is not a lack of knowledge that prevents those who are self-employed from growing their business, but rather a lack of discipline. If a self-employed person created a list of the best and most effective use of their time each day and completed everything on the list, success is all but guaranteed. Here is the remarkable difference between those employed and those self-employed. The employed person may get a % bonus at the end of the year for completing everything on the list each day. The self-employed person for doing exactly the same thing gets to keep 100% of the profits of the company and the ensuing benefits of increased productivity. Imagine the scenario where an employee was given 100% of the profits from the company he worked for. That would create some talk around the dinner table.

The question we must ask then is "What is missing for the self-employed or self-directed individual"? That's easy really. The boss. The boss is missing when you are self-employed or self-directed. Most people when asked to describe self-employment will tell you it allows you freedom, opportunity to grow and self-direction. The one thing self-employed people rarely tell you is that they have to be both the most diligent boss and the employee.

The vast majority of those who are self-employed lack the structure that exists for almost everyone in an employee/employer relationship. One person, "the boss" has the duty and obligation to plan out and delegate activity of the employee. The "employee's" job then is to carry out the tasks to the best of their ability. The system is effective and proven because there are two distinct people carrying out two separate and distinct tasks.

Here is a system that replicates the success of the corporate world. The boss/employee relationship. _Here's where the difference from most self-employed or self-directed people comes in. You have to be both boss and employee. The way that this is possible is to see yourself as two separate and distinct and people with separate obligations and responsibilities, fulfilling them at separate and distinct times of the day. Here is a structure of how and when this can be accomplished.

-1 The boss (your management side) blocks of 10-15 minutes each day and plans out the activities of the next day in complete detail in the evening for the night before.

-2 As the manager of your business or productivity, the only mandate is to structure the next day with the most effective and productive use of time. No thought is given to how the employee will view the tasks just as it is in a structured employer/employee relationship.

-3 The following morning the employee (your working side) merely picks up the schedule of activities and executes it.

It is of critical importance to realize that this is not a things to do list. Most people today operate from a list of things to do. This is a recipe for failure. Without pre-determining what tasks are to be done, when and costing out how long each will take, you will be unable to stick to the mandate of utilizing the best and most effective use of your time. Here is what happens to a typical person operating with a things to do list. They try and get as many done as they can, constantly get distracted and end up not completing key activities that will move them forward. At the end of the day, in frustration they move those tasks that were not completed to the next day. This constant wave of uncompleted tasks takes them in the wrong direction. As Jim Rohn once said, *"The difference between success and failure is this. Failure is a few errors in judgment repeated each day. Success is a disciplines repeated each day"*. The repetition of the right disciplines each day then provides the answer. There is no big bang theory. I will not succeed today and I will not fail today. Disciplines or errors in judgment will create their own corresponding outcome.

The key to planning activity with the focus on the best and most effective use of your time will come about not from a list of things to do but rather a well-crafted schedule by calendar hour. Here is the structure to consistently implement the disciplines each day that will lead to your success.

-1 At the end of each day sit down as the CEO of your life and carefully plan out the following day in complete detail by calendar hour.

-2 It is the function of The Boss to look for available time in the employee's schedule the following day. Obviously for time previously booked the boss is not going to re-arrange those commitments.

-3 In the time available, schedule those activities that will move the yardstick forward and allow the employee (you) to invest in the best and most effective use of your time the next day.

-4 Each activity must be given an appropriate amount of time to complete it. When first beginning to use this new productivity model, it is essential to grossly overestimate the amount of time you believe it will take to complete the activity. If you believe you can make 20 calls in an hour schedule 10. The key is that the employee must be provided with a sufficient amount of time to complete each task.

-5 The final key to make this work is to create a structure to manage distractions and issues that arise in the moment that we don't anticipate. Without this the entire plan will fall apart. Each day's schedule must include a buffer zone of time, one late morning and one late afternoon. This will allow you to manage situations that arise that you did not anticipate. What happens to everyone is that a phone call, e-mail or inquiry comes in and we stop doing what we had planned to deal with it. The reason being that we know we can't ignore it and so we stop our scheduled activity. This leads to a small error in judgment. Again, these small errors repeated daily will lead to failure. The buffer zone allows you a place to deal with unanticipated situations. Again, you must schedule a buffer zone late morning and late afternoon and use this time only to manage unexpected situations such as phone calls, e-mails and inquiries. By utilizing this you will be allowed to stay on task and to complete the assigned activities, which were defined by the boss as the best and most effective use of your time.

Every member of every audience I have delivered this to has said that implementing this system would at minimum double their productivity and income. With that said, the elephant is in the room. Here is a question I would like you to consider. *"What else can double your productivity and income in less than 15 minutes a day?"* The answer quite simply is nothing.

Amateurs Wing It, Professionals and Prepared Everyday

The difference between the two statements above is not what you may think. It is fascinating to realize that either outcome will simply come from your own choice.

There is a very distinct reason why some people achieve their goals and others never do. The world stands back in awe of those who seem to effortlessly accomplish what they set out to do. They are the 10-year overnight success story.

One of the greatest examples I personally witnessed of this came from an experience I had many years ago. Early on in my radio career while working at a small station, one of my co-workers was hired by a major market station in Toronto. This was the goal for us all. To make it to major market. About 2 weeks after my friend started at his new job he called and asked if I wanted to come down for a tour. I jumped at the chance. During the tour we came to the section of the station where the on-air booth was located. There was an adjacent room and seating area that allowed you to see the announcer who was on-air through the glass wall of the booth. We sat down to chat and looking through the glass of the booth I saw that the man who was on-air was "the guy". The man on-air was a legend in my business and here's why. For the 20 plus years he had been on-air no one could remember him ever making a mistake. His delivery was flawless. He never tripped over his words or stumbled which is something you will hear from almost every announcer.

While we sat talking I watched him through the glass, honest to say I was quite enamored. The speakers throughout the station carried the song he was currently playing. Through the glass I was able to see him sitting at the console writing on a notepad. He continued on with this for a few minutes and then put the notepad on the lectern in front of him. Then I could see his mouth move (given that he was in a soundproof booth) but the song continued to play. A couple of minutes later the song began to wind down, the red light came on outside of the booth indicating he was live on-air and we heard him say,

"That was U2 and One on 104.5 CHUM FM, I'm (his name) it's 2:23 in the afternoon, 59 degrees going to a high later today of 64. Clear tonight and back up to 70 tomorrow. Don't forget to be listening tomorrow morning to Roger, Rick and Marilyn for the sound of the Chum Fm jet, your chance to win a trip for two down to beautiful sunny Barbados. 2:24 now, coming up Maria Carey and Bryan Adams on the way, I'm (his name) on CHUM Fm".

With that he went into the commercial break. Once the commercials were finished he introduced the next song and left the booth to go to the washroom. My friend said, *"C'mom, I'll show you the booth"*. Stepping inside the booth was everything I had imagined. The best equipment money could buy and the logo of CHUM FM, emblazoned in the wall. While looking around I saw the notepad he had been writing on. Curious, I looked around to make certain he was not returning and read what he had written. I was floored. On the notepad was every single word he had just said, including his name! In that moment I found out that he was not a legend. He was not a god. He was just a pro. What he had been doing for 20 plus years was this. Every time he spoke on-air, he thought out in advance what he was going to say, then wrote out every word and then put the notepad in front of him and read it out loud two or three times. After that he turned on the microphone and delivered it perfectly.

In that moment I realized that we all have the ability to function at that level. The lesson that day was this. On the days you want amateur results, wing it. On the days you want professional results, be a pro. The fascinating realization is that how our lives turn out most times comes down to little more than choice. We all have the choice to show up every day and act as a pro, or we can choose to fumble through and wing it. Here is the truth then. On the days you want professional results you have to be a pro. Right now. Right in this moment make the decision to be a pro. Skill and good looks will get you through some days. Being prepared 'EVERYDAY' is the answer to continued growth and success. Coming up we'll discuss the process and magic of relationships. Before that; the story of the boy who climbed to the heavens.

Into the Heavens and Beyond

A s a boy, he had a dream to one-day soar into the heavens. He had no way of knowing the path he would have to follow or the fact that his journey into the skies would be one grueling step at a time, straight up the tallest mountain in the world.

You may not have heard of him, but his story is one of the most remarkable and inspiring I've ever heard. I met him through a radio interview I did a few years ago. His name is Sean Swarner. He grew up in the small town of Willard, Ohio, population 5,000. His childhood was normal, fun and uneventful. His father, the local dentist, had a big heart and would often provide services to his clients who couldn't afford them in exchange for vegetables. *"There was no lack of vegetables on our table growing up,"* he said.

He was fascinated with space and with the heavens. Seeing his passion, his parents decided to help him realize his dream and send him to space camp when he was 13. But it was a trip Sean was never able to make. Before he could leave for camp, he fell ill. *"I was going up for a layup in basketball when something snapped in my knee. A couple days later, the injury caused every joint in my body to swell up,"* he said.

Initially, Sean was treated at a local hospital for what was thought to be pneumonia. After further concerns were raised, he was transferred to a larger hospital in Columbus, Ohio. It was there that the diagnosis was made: Sean had Hodgkin's lymphoma. His parents were told that the disease was already in the fourth stage, and he was given just three months to live. At the time, they didn't tell Sean, because his step grandmother had just died of cancer two months before.

The aggressive chemotherapy and steroid treatment lasted for more than a year. He lost all his hair, and his normally fit body ballooned 60 pounds because of the steroids. Sean said, *"There were nights that, when I went to bed, I didn't know if I was going to wake up in the morning. My mom and dad slept on the floor right next to me."*

For most teenagers, school is an ongoing popularity contest, and the challenges presented by not only his illness but his looks were difficult for Sean to face.

After only two months into the treatment, Sean was determined to fight with everything he had and began a fitness program. One of his other passions was swimming, and two months before the treatment was finished, Sean insisted that the Hickman catheter be pulled from his chest so he could compete in the summer-league championship swim meet. Against the wishes of his parents and coaches, Sean achieved his goal: He entered the meet and finished the race. Not winning the race was hard for Sean – he'd never lost a race in the summer league. But the most important goal was reached: to make it up and back, to live. He did that and more. At the end of his treatment, Sean was finally given a clean bill of health and was able to resume the normal life of a teenager.

Then a year later, during a checkup, he was hit with another obstacle. *"They found a golf ball-size tumor on my right lung,"* he said. This time doctors gave him only 14 days to live. It was a rare form of cancer called Askin's sarcoma. *"And that's when I lost it. I went back to the bed, stuck my face in the pillow and just started crying,"* he said.

The radiation treatment that ensued damaged most of his right lung. Further treatment included daily chemotherapy and radiation for a month, followed by 10 more months of chemotherapy. Remember, they had given Sean fourteen days to live?

Sean is a living medical miracle. He's the only known person in recorded medical history to have had – let alone survived -- both Hodgkin's lymphoma and Askin's sarcoma. The illnesses left him with only one fully functioning lung, but his obstacles also gave him a new purpose in life.

"My goal is to inspire others to motivate themselves," he said.

To do that he set his sights on the highest mountain in the world: Mount Everest.

"Most of the outfitters told me that there's no way they'd take a one-lung, two-time cancer-survivor lunatic up the highest mountain in the world," he said.

On Everest, he faced 100-mph winds, snowstorms, deadly avalanches and a significant loss of oxygen. -- hazards that challenge even the most accomplished climbers. *"And the Sherpas were kind of scared, too, because in Nepal there's no such thing as a cancer survivor,"* he said. Another tragedy struck Sean on the climb when he lost one of his best friends, a fellow climber on the trip.

.

For Sean, taking on Everest was a lot like fighting cancer. *"Everyone has their own Everest to climb. And everyone is battling their own mountains, and fighting cancer and going through treatments is an uphill struggle"* he said.

Sean is the only known cancer survivor to have reached the summit of Mount Everest. He believes the body can accomplish anything the mind can dream. And who would argue? He's living proof that a positive mental attitude truly can take you to new heights. *"If a two-time cancer survivor with one lung can climb the highest mountain in the world, anybody can do anything they want to,"* he said.

He said one his favorite things to do is to visit kids with cancer after each of his climbs. He loves lifting their spirits. But he also said that's one of the hardest things he does. When he walks into an oncology ward, it brings back a flood of memories from when he was in their shoes. Still, his visits are an inspiration to both the kids and their families.

Through his passion to take his message of hope to others suffering with cancer, Sean started the Cancer Climber Association. The nonprofit group organizes events to raise money for kids with cancer. They do event runs, safaris and expeditions up mountains such as Kilimanjaro and donate the money to that camps to support them so children with cancer can escape their lives for a while and realize how much there is to live for.

Sean's dream and his passion to make a difference in the lives of those affected by cancer live on. You can visit him on the Web to make donations, get more information or book Sean for speaking engagements, at www.seanswarner.com or www.cancerclimber.org.

For reasons most will never understand, Sean was put on this Earth to inspire others and to prove that anything is possible. He made a decision long ago to simply help others. To him it has never been work. There is no question that every week he is *"Looking Forward to Monday's"*.

8

Relationships

Relationships are the cornerstone of business and life. We all have had the experience of seeing others who appear to be natural masters at relationships. They are people we often refer to as 'charismatic'. Charisma is evidenced through the delivery of the key aspects of relationship development on autopilot. Those who appear to be charismatic have become masters at the art, often through the impact of parents or positive personal re-enforcement from their own early interactions with others. Anyone can become a master at relationships. Anyone can learn the process of what is required to create great relationships and through practice and implementation become masters themselves. The absolute in business has remained constant throughout history. Here is the key and something that every successful businessperson will attest to. People do not do business with the brightest or most experienced. People do business with people that they like and trust. The answer then to explode our business and life potential is to learn this skill and become a master at relationships.

No doubt we are a complicated species but the first and most important element to understand about relationship development can be found in the answer to this question. *"What is the most important topic of discussion for any person on the planet?"* The answer is one of the fastest I ever get in seminars. *"Themselves"!*

The first step in understanding the keys to relationship development then is to begin with the knowledge that a critical component inherent in all of us is that everyone wants to matter. Everyone wants to belong. No one wants to feel invisible. Most make the mistake of believing that it is their skill and knowledge that will make the difference and thus make the connection. While knowledge is certainly important, making a connection on an emotional level is the key to open all doors.

In seminars I often tell of an experience I had while in radio that had a lasting and profound affect on me with two of the members of the band Aerosmith. As often is the case when bands or entertainers want to promote a new album or tour, they will hold a private party and invite the key members of the media. The idea being that each member of the media is a connector and as such has the power to relay the message out to tens of thousands of listeners and viewers and readers.

On this particular day we were invited to attend an album listening party for Aerosmith. It was held at a local nightclub over the lunch hour (closed to invitation only) and all members of the local media were in attendance. It is important to preface this by saying that the media are a spoiled lot. We were given free passes and merchandise almost daily with the hope of a message being passed on to the public. Read, *"free advertising"*. Again, for the majority of the members of the media who were there that day the real reason we showed up was for the free lunch, free merchandise and to get a chance to meet and mingle with our friends.

Given that we all had regular access few were interested in actually meeting the band. In most cases the band stayed in the back room and would come out for a couple of minutes to wave hello before being shuttled off to their hotel rooms.

This day was different and one I will never forget. While standing at the bar chatting with friends, the two lead members of the band came out of the back room and made their way to the middle of the bar. I saw them come out but then turned back to my conversation. In a few moments I heard some commotion from the middle of the bar and turned to see a few reporters around them. Stephen Tyler picked up one of the female reporters and was posing for pictures. Again, I went back to my conversation. When I turned back I saw something that almost never happened. A line-up was forming to meet these two. Again, the members of the media are spoiled and never line up. Within about 10 minutes I broke ranks with my past and I was in the line-up.

Soon the entire collection of media people was in a line-up that snaked around the entire club. Standing in line I began to try and come up with what I hoped would be the perfect question. An answer I would share with my listeners later in the day when I was on-air. It took about 45 minutes before I made my way to the front of the line. Armed with my question I shot out my hand and Stephen Tyler took over.

"Hey man, how are you doing? What's your name?" I told him and his barrage of questions continued, *"What station do you work at? What music do you like to listen to? Do you meet chicks?"* The astounding thing that happened was

that for five minutes he interviewed me. He shone the light on me. He was interested in me. I walked away realizing too late that I never had a chance to ask my question.

The magic of these two became instantly apparent. Even though they were international superstars, had been in the business for 30 years and sold over 50 million albums they still recognized the importance of connecting to the people they meet and making them feel like they mattered. This promotional appearance became a day we will all remember. At the end of the hour an a half 150 of the top media people in the country could not wait to get back to our listeners and viewers and readers to tell them what great guys they were and how amazing the album was. (I'm not sure if I even heard it) Here is the key then. Regardless of where you are or who you become make certain to know that the light must be shone on the one you are looking to create a relationship with.

The next step in relationship development is to become a master at listening. There is no question that much is written about the art of listening and sayings like *"you have two ears and one mouth so listen twice as much as you talk"* are common but putting this skill into practice takes focus and well, practice.

Here is what being a good listener tells the one you are looking to connect with. You care about them. You find them interesting. You are shining the light on them and allowing them to engage in the most interesting conversation they will ever have, which as was pointed out is themselves.

While staying entirely focused on the conversation of another is a challenge for us all, that focus in a personal relationship situation is linked to one very important element. That is fear. The definition of fear is that *"I am here and I want to be there."* In this case, the "here" is in the early stages of communication with another. The "there" is the place you want to be to know if you have provided enough information and proven your value to such an extent that it will lead to an expanded relationship and ultimately business or personal gain. This "fear" is responsible for your mind constantly racing ahead of the conversation searching for the next probing question or comment that will win the other over.

By doing this, you are disconnecting with the other and missing out on what they wanted all along. To be heard. To know that you are listening and that they matter. Taking the time to listen and blocking out that mental magnet that pulls you out of the moment will show another that you really care about where they are now and what matters to them.

The person you are looking to connect with will know you are listening by your response and interaction. When they are telling you about their family or job or personal interests or experiences being a keen listener will allow you to follow along and ask the next probing question about their interest or experience.

Johnny Carson was the quintessential master at this. Johnny was without question the king of late night talk shows. To the viewer it may not have appeared that he had a plan or set philosophy but there is no question that he did. He actually wrote about it in a book called "The Green Room" that is no longer in print. In the book he detailed his approach to the show. When he was doing his monologue or a skit the light shone on him. When he sat with a guest he made the switch and completely focused the light on them. If a guest sat down and Johnny began to ask him about their latest project and they veered off to tell him about some strange thing that happened in their life, Johnny's questions went out the window and he 100% focused on what they were saying and stayed with the topic. This focus and ability to listen and shine the light made his show magic to watch. He was the king of late night television not by charm and good looks but by having a set philosophy that relationships were everything. As a result he was able to get guests to share personal aspects of their lives that no others were privy to. The end result was great television.

Learning to quiet the mind and be at ease in the infant stage of relationship development is key. After interviewing thousands of people over more than twenty years in radio and television one of the most important skills I learned was the ability to put people at ease. A great deal of the people I interviewed over the years had never been before a microphone or camera before and had great anxiety and trepidation about the experience. Remember, the #1 fear after death is public speaking.

What I found to be the most helpful was to first set their mind at ease and tell them that we were just going to have a conversation and ask them a number of simple questions before we went to air to warm them up. The second, and most critical advice was to instill in them the knowledge that whatever it was they were there to talk about, without question they were the expert. If I had an expert guest on my show to talk about their area of expertise, the reality was that there would be no trick questions. If they were a doctor or lawyer or business leader or writer they were the elephant in the room.

The same holds true for your experience with another. Know that while you are in conversation in business you are the expert. If you are the one looking to provide the product or service you likely have years of experience in that one focused area. Take comfort in the fact that in your meeting this knowledge is something that should serve and not hinder you. What I find to be the greatest detractor from listening is that people enter meetings and carry in the baggage of dozens of questions in their mind that they hope to ask. Doing that will all but guarantee that you do not listen. What happens too often is that the person you are meeting with will make an important point and you will fail to react or follow up because your mind had raced ahead to the next question. The answer is to shut it out. Relax. Remember, your number one priority in the early stages of relationship development is to listen and respond to the person you are looking to connect with you. Doing this tells the person you are interested in them and you care. Miss this and your questions will serve no purpose because the truth is that you are not going to do business with them or anyone until you connect and begin to create a relationship.

The next step in relationship development is to find out what they want and what solution you can provide to improve their situation. The delivery of a product or service is always connected to filling a need and solving a problem. Ultimately, the client is looking for an experience to be fulfilled. They may want peace of mind to travel in retirement, improved productivity leading to success, a better car to enjoy the drive or a new home where a family can create memories.

The transition to the next stage of relationship development then is to switch gears from shining the light to needs and wants discovery. Here is what I suggest to clients. "Mr. or Mrs. ?, I am always fascinated to find out how my product (or service) will impact people. If you were to have (? Product or service) how would you hope it would improve your life and what would improve? Most in business believe when a specific item is desired they know the client and can move in for the close. Unfortunately what is almost always missed is the final step. This is illustrated in the story of the drill.

The story goes that I decide one day to go to Home Depot to purchase a drill. It is an amazing place for men to visit, given that it is full of tools and smells like wood. I take my time in the tool department and carefully select a Black and Decker ¾" variable speed, cordless drill. The price tag is $149.95. I happily line up at the cash, pay for it, put it into a bag and take it out to my car. On the ride home at a stoplight I open the bag to have a look at it and the receipt falls out. Looking down I realize, now quite upset that this may be one of the dumbest purchases I've ever made. Why did I do this? I didn't want a drill. I've never wanted a drill. You see I wanted holes but they don't sell holes so I had to buy the drill.

That is the final and most important step in relationship development that almost everyone misses. They fail to find out what the holes are. Here is an example of the final stage. If I were a financial advisor and I was working with a client to discover what truly mattered in their life, I may find out that the client is an avid fisherman. Asking the question, *"Is this something that you would want to continue into retirement and what would improve it for them?,* the client reveals they have long had a dream of owning a championship bass boat. For most discovering that what the client really wanted was this great boat, they would then believe they knew the trigger and move in for the close. Again, this is one step short of completing the process. The boat you see is the drill. Your job is to find out what the holes are.

Taking it that one extra step you are to ask the client, *"Let's assume that we are able to afford the boat in retirement. Describe for me what a day's fishing would be like"?* The client may say, *"Well, I would get up early at around 4:30 in the morning. Pack our lunch and snacks and drinks into the car. Hook up the boat and go and pick up my friend. By the time we get to the lake and launch the boat the sun would just be coming up. At that time of the day its so beautiful. The mist is just burning off the water, we are casting out catching bass and telling all the lies and jokes we have since we were kids".* Bang! That's the hole. When the client described the scene to you, you saw it. When they did, they also saw it and more importantly they felt it. As a result they would have the emotional response to the perceived experience.

One of the most powerful tools to relationship building is to be present and responsible for an emotional connection with others. Especially positive ones. We have heard the stories and seen the images of the kitten that is orphaned and adopted by a family dog. When the newborn kitten's eyes first open and that dog provides the first sense of comfort, the kitten will forever associate that emotion with who is there. In this case the family dog. That connection is so strong that for many kittens they begin to believe they are dogs as well.

When all steps are followed in relationship development you too will become a master at creating relationships. Maya Angelou wrote the following words many years ago and they are absolutely true. She said;

"People will forget what you did

and forget what you said

but they will never forget how you made them feel"

Self-Analysis Exercise

The best and most effective way to learn is through practice and testing. The following is a self-analysis exercise to use to engrain the steps of the process into the sub-conscious mind. Following each interaction, take the time and score yourself on how you did ensuring that you included the following.

-1 Shine the light

Begin the building of any relationship by engaging in conversation about points of interest for the person you are meeting with.

-2 Listen/Respond

When they begin to tell you something of themselves, make certain to listen and respond. Continue the line of communication for a few minutes to show them that you are generally interested in their lives. Make certain to focus and not become distracted by an agenda you bring in with you.

-3 Needs/wants discovery

This is where you begin to discover their triggers for working with you. Ask them what would happen and how their lives would be improved through your product or service?

-4 Show the movie

The final step may be the most important and the least invested in. Once you find out what is truly important to them, ask them to tell you what it will be like and to describe the experience of having it. When you get them to show you the movie in their mind of what they really want and have an emotional connection to it they will become your client and make the connection.

9

The Power of Why

New client acquisition has always and remains one of the most important activities and greatest challenges in business. Changing our approach to the marketplace is the keys to not only reduce the number of contacts necessary to secure a new client but also to differentiate ourselves from competitors in the marketplace. This new approach I am suggesting can and will be a game changer in your growth and success.

The reality is that almost every corporation or individual present their product or service to the marketplace in this way.

- Here is *what* I do. (this defines the appropriate market sector)

- Here is *how* I do it. (this proposes to differentiate their product or process from the competition)

The challenge of this approach is that you are very limited in what differentiates you from the competition. An example of one business sector is the financial services industry. It is estimated here in Canada that there are over 80,00 finance professionals. Given the level of competition it stands to reason that if the vast majority are presenting themselves to potential clients in very much the same way, standing out and providing a competitive edge becomes the differentiator between success and failure. The problem I see far to often is that we get so close to our product or service that we make the critical mistake of assuming a potential client will see the difference in our process and want to do business with us based on that. The reality is that the public rarely takes note of the difference and nuance of one to another. As we discussed in the chapter on relationships, people don't do business with the brightest or most experienced. People do business with people that they like and trust. Business then is built on relationships.

One other major element of the challenge of the standard approach, "Hi I'm Randy. Here is what I do and how I do it" is that this is an approach focused on business. The problem is that it is a fact of human nature that we all have a fear of being sold and as such put up a protective layer between ourselves and the person who is looking to do business with us. I was told a story a number of year ago of a businessperson who goes to a client's door. At the door he stops and reads the following sign. *"No sales people or solicitation allowed."* The question is "what does the sign mean". Most would say that perhaps the person is very busy or has been bothered by too many sales people in the past. The reality is, that's not it. What the sign really means is *"Please don't ring my doorbell, I buy everything"*. Again the truth is that people do business with people they like and trust. If these are absolutes, and they are, why then would we start on business? The answer is to completely alter our approach to new clients and share "why" we do what we do.

Your "why" is unique only to you and defines what makes you different.

Let me explain. Your 'why' is what you take from the process of working with your clients that creates an emotional response for you. Everyone understands and knows that you make a living doing what you do. The way to set yourself apart is to share why you do what you do that has nothing to do with the income you derive from it. I have heard it too many times from business people that they believe a prospect just wants to get down to business and is not interested in why you do what you do. Nothing could be further from the truth. New prospective clients will not do business with you until they make a connection and begin to develop a relationship. Remember, they have to like and trust you. Sharing what you get from the work you do with clients on an emotional level will accomplish that and again set you apart from the competition.

I should point out that this is not something that is new. Some of the top corporations and individuals in the world have adopted this approach and have become market and world leaders. They don't follow the masses and go out into the marketplace promoting what they do and how they do it. They very clearly define their 'why' and communicate it effectively to potential customers. It is proven through science that there is a limited emotional connection to a product, service or process. These attributes are processed by the logical portion of our brain. Presenting to the marketplace the reason *why* we do what we do appeals to the emotional zone of the brain and has a far greater impact on interest leading to the creation of a connection. Connection = business.

Bose audio is a great example of a corporation who followed this philosophy and has ended up dominating their market sector. I was fascinated to witness their approach first hand. A few years ago my wife gave me a Bose audio system for father's day. When I opened the box, sitting on top was a simple slip of paper that displays their corporate philosophy and mission statement. Here is what was written on the paper, At Bose Audio we are driven *to creating the finest audio experience possible. To that end we re-invest 100% of corporate profits back into research and development"*. When I share this with audiences I ask them "Where did you see or hear the words woofer or tweeter or harmonic distortion? Take note of the fact that the phrase they used was, "Audio EXPERIENCE". They did not say audio components or products or widgets or price, but *experience*. This is their "why". This is why they exist. There is something we can all learn from this. What "experience" are you looking to create for your clients and what drives you personally? What do you take away from the process emotionally? What is your why? Defining it and sharing it with the marketplace makes you different. It truly is a game changer.

Apple Computers is another classic example. Apple is seen by the world as the leaders in computing technology. They compete in an arena where the differentiation of advantages has long been the focus of competition. Here is how the majority of computer manufacturers vie for market share. "My machine is faster than your machine. My machine can do this. My machine does what the others do but costs less". A long time ago Steve Jobs and the folks at Apple made the decision to have another approach. They decided not to go to the marketplace and state not what they do and how they do it. They broke away from the competition when they began to tell the consumer why they existed. They said, *"We are driven to simplify your experience with technology. We want to make computers that are easy to use"*.

Read the words, *"simplify your experience."* Those are words of purpose and passion. Those words are Apple computers "*Why*". Steve Jobs and his team knew that more than anything, the typical consumer was not so motivated by price as they were by wanting a machine they could easily use and that would not make them feel inferior or incapable. Apple tapped into this with their "why". Are there other companies in the exact same business? Of course. What makes them different not only in words but in actions that stem from that, *"Driven to simplify your experience with technology"*.

In seminars I often use the example of the advertising piece that was created for Apple back in the late 1990's. At the time Jobs and his team were working with an ad firm trying to come up with something that would identify their vision and set them apart from the competition. What came of that search was one of the most iconic pieces of advertising in our history. The words not only define the vision of the company but are also fantastic words to live by. Here they are.

"Here's to the crazy ones. The misfits. The rebels. The troublemakers. The round pegs in the square holes. The ones who see things differently. They're not fond of rules. And they have no respect for the status quo. You can quote them, disagree with them, glorify or vilify them. About the only thing you can't do is ignore them. Because they change things. They invent. They imagine. They heal. They explore. They create. They inspire. They push the human race forward. While some see them as the crazy ones, we see genius. Because the people who are crazy enough to think they can change the world, are the ones who do".

I normally read these words out loud and then ask the audience as I will you. Where did you see the words dual core processor? Speed? Price? Competitive advantage? You don't. The words you see above have nothing to do with what they do or how they do it. Apple computers set themselves apart and now dominate the computer industry because they were able to share with consumers 'why' they do what they do.

It is not only corporations who have had tremendous success with this philosophical approach. A great many individuals have created great success and even altered the course of history by letting others know their 'why' rather than their what and how. Back in the 1960's during the tragic days of the race riots one man rose above the violence and oppression to have his voice heard. In just 17 minutes Martin Luther King pushed forward the wheels of change with a speech delivered on August 28th, 1963 on the steps of the Lincoln Memorial.

As U.S. Representative John Lewis said of his iconic speech,

"Dr. King had the power, the ability, and the capacity to transform those steps on the Lincoln Memorial into a monumental area that will forever be recognized. By speaking the way he did, he educated, he inspired, he informed not just the people there, but people throughout America and unborn generations."

During his 17 minutes he did not tell the crowd what he or they were going to do. He did not share with them or try and convince them that he had a plan to overcome the violence and inequality. Dr. King did something that was rooted in the name of his speech. *"I have a dream"* he said. In essence what he said was *"I have a why"*. *"Here is why I do this"* Dr.

King said, *"Because I have a dream"*. His why was the dream that one day all of God's children, black and white would join hands and live in harmony. More than 200,000 people showed up at the Lincoln Memorial because they were inspired by his dream.

When you look back at the impact his words and his 'why' had that day you can see again the power of why. Dr. King's why was so great and so powerful that his words reverberated around the square and around the city and around the state and the nation and the world with such force that as we sit here today less than 50 years later a black man has taken up residence for a second term in a house that was built by slaves. How powerful was his why? This is what we all need to do. To inspire others with our dream and the reason why we do what we do. It's the place where emotions live. It's a connection that can't be quantified or denied or compared to. It's your own. It's what makes you, you.

The exercise is to create your own, *"I have a dream speech"*. By doing this and altering your approach to the marketplace you will accomplish two dramatic things. One, your initial approach with new clients will not be based on business, causing them to pull back in a protective way but will allow you to begin to start where all business ends which is on relationships. Two, it will set you apart from all other competitors and make you different. It will make you real and will enlighten your prospect with the driving force in your life far beyond money that keeps you doing what you do.

There is one caveat to the process of creating your why that I would like to be very honest with you about. This is going to take time and energy and patience to get it right. It is absolutely essential to follow the prescribed detailed steps of the process below. If you try and rush it and skip over steps of the process I can tell you that it won't go well.

Here are the steps to create and ultimately deliver your "why". Again, this is not a 5-minute process and will take time. Perhaps several days or weeks. The end result in new business development will be substantial. Here are the necessary steps to ensure that your 'why' is well thought out, rehearsed and delivered.

-1 Define your "why". Your why is the emotional connection that you have that is unique to yourself in the execution of your job. Aside from the money, what drives you emotionally to create what you do with your clients.

-2 Next provide an example or story that illustrates your why.

-3 Then begin to script your why in written form, re-writing it as many times as is necessary so that the words are just the way you speak. For many this will replace your so called 'elevator speech'.

-4 Finally, and this is a critical last step, rehearse your script out loud over and over until the words flow and sound like your own. Then and only then are you ready to deliver your "why".

-5 When someone asks you what you do, tell them why. That is what will make you different.

Since I began teaching this years ago, the list of my own clients who adopted this has grown and so have their results. I hear it from my own clients over and over what a dramatic difference this has made in their business development efforts. One final point I would like to make about defining why you do what you do is the impact this will have on you. All of us looking to provide a product or service to the marketplace are in one way or another involved in the world of sales. Something I hear from clients over and over is that they don't want to feel like a salesman. They want to distance themselves from that negative connotation not only for their clients but themselves as well. Sharing your why will do just that. Both you and your client will know that money is not the main driving force for you being there. There is another reason much more important and more valuable. It is 'your why'.

10

The bridge or the cliff?

This chapter will deal with creating and defining the plan to make your goal possible. There are two ways to get to where you want to be. Given that you are not likely starting from a place in your life void of responsibilities there will be aspects of your life to take into consideration. Most, when considering a change stop short of beginning the process because they can't see their way clear to how to even start. Know that the approach to any change in our lives has options. You can choose either the bridge or the cliff. If you are looking to make major changes, the bridge will allow for you to stay in your current position or on your current path while you slowly transition to your new chosen direction. The cliff provides for a total and complete break from where you are to enter through the door to where you want to go. Both are possible. Both offer positives. Both harbor potential pitfalls.

We'll begin with the cliff. This choice and philosophy harkens back to the days of the Greeks. Ancient Greek warriors were some of the toughest fighters in history. It wasn't so much their training or their weapons or their tactics. It was their philosophy and unwavering commitment to win. When they would arrive on enemy shores, the first orders from their commanders would be to "burn the ships." And they did. The message was loud and clear: there was no turning back. There was no retreat. No surrender. The only way out was forward. Victory or death. They would entertain no other outcome. This is the way of the cliff. When you have identified what your goals and passion are in life and what direction you want to take, the cliff provides providence for you to burn the ships. It may mean quitting a job. Selling a home. Moving to another part of the city or country or world. Choosing the cliff is an exhilarating free fall, clinging to the belief on the way down that an updraft will catch you and allow you to soar back up into the skies.

I heard some great advice while watching American Idol a couple of years ago. One of the contestants was asked what advice they had received along the way through the competition. She said that she had met the lead singers from a very popular band backstage and she asked if he had any advice to give to someone new into the business. Without hesitation he said, *"Yeah, don't have a plan "B"*. Once you have found your passion, there is only one direction. Straight forward.

The Cliff

Benefits

- o Clean break
- o Maximum time available to invest on your new life
- o Absolute commitment to your decision

Challenges

- o Income

- o Support from family and friends

- o Shorter window for initial success before challenges take over

The Bridge

The bridge is your second option and frankly one that most choose to take. The bridge sets your plan in motion while allowing you to stay on in your current path. The bridge allows for obvious benefits but it also provides for challenges that hide beneath the surface.

Benefits

- o Steady income from your current position
- o Added time to research your plan of action
- o Ability to keep your new passion and goal to yourself and avoid negative input

Challenges

- o Possible decision to back out
- o Limited time to invest in new move
- o Difficulty in hiding your potential move from loved ones

My own experience took advantage of both the cliff and the bridge. When I decided to jump into broadcasting in 1983 at $4.25 an hour I chose the cliff. The predominant reason was that I was presented with an opportunity that may have gone away had I wanted to stay on the bridge. I was offered a job as a part time radio announcer while working as a sales rep for a fortune 500 company. At the time I was making very good money, drove a company car, had a family to support and was doing well. I knew I couldn't do both and so I jumped. To make it happen I sold my car. Bought an old beater and took any and every part time sales and manual labor job that allowed the flexibility to work the shifts I was offered. I had no way of knowing when I began but this part time frenzied life would last for a year and three months before I was offered a full time slot. Even when I did get fulltime I was making about ¼ of what I did at my sales job. At the end of my career in radio I was making 5x what I made in sales. The world rewards those who follow their heart.

The next change in my life came in 2002 when I left broadcasting to enter this field of personal and professional development. Looking back I would say that what I did was somewhat of a hybrid. I half walked across the bridge and half jumped. I knew this was what I wanted to do a very long time ago. I felt I needed to prove my theory of following your dreams and needed to wait until I made it to the top in my field. I also used the last year and a half to put my thoughts together and to write a book before leaving broadcasting. When I left that was all I had. There were no clients and no testimonials. The coaching programs I have created were still dormant seeds that would not even hatch for 2 more years. I wanted to speak and I wanted to help others find their dreams and potential and I believed in the power of my dream.

The ride in the early going was exhilarating and more than occasionally scary. There were times when I questioned if I was doing the right thing. There were times when I wondered if I was putting my family's future at risk. There were times when I doubted. What I will tell you is that every time I got down and started to question my decision I imagined what my life would be like if I went back to a job of just trading life for money. It was that image and the impending sadness and defeat that kept pushing me forward. In the moment it was a challenge. Looking back from where I sit today I can tell you that without question it was the right thing to do. Once your have your vision of where you want to go, think this through as to which path is right for you and then set about the business of making it happen.

The decision of which direction to take reminds me of a story I tell often during seminars. It's the story of five seagulls one day who are sitting on the railing of a pier that juts out into the ocean. It is a beautiful day. The sun is shining and the boats are coming and going out of the harbor. The gulls sit watching the boats and the clouds and the ocean wash in and out. Finally one of the gulls decides to get up and leave. The question is *"how many seagulls are left"?* The answer almost always is four. You would think so but the correct answer is five. You see he *decided* to leave but never actually went anywhere. Make certain that you are not like the seagull that decides to embark on your new life of passion and purpose but never spreads their wings. Get up off the railing and fly.

Oprah Winfrey marked the end of 25 years of broadcasting with a final show that featured no special guests. No big prize giveaways. No surprises. It was just her and an audience sharing her thoughts of the experience and what she had learned over the 25 years. The key to her message was asking and pleading with her loyal viewers to find their calling in life. She noted that hers was the stage of a television show. Another may be to teach and inspire children or paint or sing or write or train dogs. *"Find what you love and do that"* was her message.

When sitting down to map out your goals and create your plan it is common to feel that there is so little you know about where you want to be and so few skills that you possess that will be required to climb your mountain. Here is what you need know. You have the skills. You have everything inside of you at this moment in time to become or have or go anywhere in this world. The skills you have and the level of knowledge may need polishing and refining and strengthening but make no mistake that you are not without them. Think about this. If you wanted to become healthier would you know that you would need to eat better? If you wanted to meet a person would you have the words to introduce yourself? If you wanted to become an astronaut would you understand there is education you will need to take in order to qualify? The answer is yes. Given that, there is a simple process involved to have or become anything.

Identify

    Research

        Implement

            Rehearse.

This is the process that separates a bus driver from a neurosurgeon. What most don't understand is that the bus driver is a neurosurgeon without training. The skills exist inside of him. They only need to be polished. Everything we have done in life has made it possible for us to arrive at where we are today. Beginning with the ability to walk and talk. Tie our shoes. To read and write, to drive a car and to function in our personal lives and in the business world. Consider for a moment, all that you have learned to date that has made possible who you are at this moment? This realization will open the door and shine the light on what is possible for you if you continue to learn and grow and polish the God given abilities that exist inside of you right now. Know that the commitment to continue to grow will allow you to achieve your dream. Any dream.

Mapping out a concrete plan of what you must do and what you must learn to arrive at your destination is the key to all of this. As Jim Rohn said, *"Aspiration without perspiration is a recipe for delusion"*. Consider this. If you set out on a journey without a map you would just wander aimlessly and likely never arrive at your destination. When I was 18 years old I decided on a dare to drive from Toronto to California. The bet was that we would not be able to make it in less than two days. We arrived in just over 47 hours and I collected the $10. wager. If we had not picked up a map and planned out our route we may still be driving today. There is no real way of getting to your destination without a map. A plan not only includes the steps of how you will get there but also the commitment of purpose. Saying you are going to do it is the start. Planning how you will do it is the next step. Taking action and following the plan is the fuel that completes the journey. There will be many twists and turns along the way but following this simple philosophy will make it all possible.

There are fascinating stories throughout history that pay homage to the power of the plan. Some are extremely detailed and complicated. Other are a simple commitment to purpose. Andrew Carnegie was a Scottish-American industrialist, businessman and entrepreneur who was the cornerstone in the late nineteenth century of the expansion of the American steel industry.

Carnegie's fortune was estimated at four hundred and fifty million dollars - the equivalent to four and a half billion dollars today. In addition to building Carnegie Hall in New York City, he founded libraries in hundreds of small towns all across America and participated in dozens of other philanthropic activities as well.

When he died a note was found in his desk drawer that he wrote when he was a young man that said this, *"I am going to spend the first half of my life accumulating money, and I am going to spend the last half of my life giving it all away."* A very simple plan and a goal that once identified held him to his promise and propelled him to his destination.

Another fascinating example of the power of a goal and written plan came from the country of Japan. It was in 1950, when struggling to recover from the ravages of war they set a goal carved out between government and industry to become the number one country in the world for textiles. By 1960, just a brief 10 years later they had achieved it. Then in 1960 they set another goal. This, far loftier than the last. They set the goal and predicted that they would become the number one producer of steel in the world. To the world it seemed impossible given that they had no iron ore of their own and as such would have to import every ounce of it. They also had no coal to power the factories to produce it. By 1970 they had achieved it and had become the number one producer of steel in the world.

Choosing not to sit and settle for past success, their next goal was set in the 1970's to become the world leader in the production of automobiles. This was a goal and prediction they missed. Not by much. They missed the target by just one year. Then finally in 1980 they set the goal to be the #1 nation in the world in the production of computers. And they did.

Setting the goal and then planning the process does two very important things. First and foremost it provides structure and a map to follow towards the destination. The second benefit is that it creates a defined purpose. During the primaries in the U.S. federal election, then candidate Barak Obama quoted Dr. King when he spoke of *"the fierce urgency of now".* *"If not now then when"?* Was his question. It is so easy to get faked out into accepting the notion that we will begin this *"soon"* or we will start *"tomorrow".* Know this. The world is littered with the lost stories of those who put off doing what would have provided an extraordinary life to tomorrow. In order to arrive at your destination you must begin. Don't lose sight of the fierce urgency of now. Tomorrow has a way of becoming never.

That is exactly what writing your goal and mapping out your plan does. It makes it real. It makes it tangible. It begins to transfer thought into substance. It begins to paint the brushstrokes on the canvas that will one day become your masterpiece. Having a written plan also gives you focus and drive. When you have transitioned from thought to seeing it written down on paper it becomes motivating, exciting and tangible. This is what will drive you to begin to invest in the activity that is necessary to succeed.

We hear a great deal of discussion in society today about the value of leadership. Leadership itself stems from first developing self-leadership. What the greatest leaders in all walks of life do so well is to articulate their vision and then assist their people to understand it, buy into the target, follow along the path and then agree to co-create throughout the process.

If you change your goals and map out your plan you will change your life. The truth is that most people today have goals and at the least framework of a plan. For too many however the goal is to keep the job they are uninspired by. The goal is to try and keep up with credit card debt. The goal is to keep the house clean, to get the shopping done and to walk the dog. Maintaining these goals and staying on this path is primarily driven by fear. The fear that this is all there is and to deviate from it would spell disaster and failure. Clinging to these goals will without question create a life. Just not the one you are deserving of.

Jim Rohn told the story many times of an early conversation with his mentor Earl Sheoff. They had just met and Jim Rohn was 25 years old and was not doing well. Mr. Sheoff asked, *"How are you doing Mr. Rohn"*. To which he replied, *"Not very well. I'm behind on my bills and behind on my promises to my family"*. Mr. Sheoff looked at him and said, *"How long have you been doing this Mr. Rohn"?* He thought for a moment and replied. *"About 5 years sir"*. To that Mr. Sheoff replied, *"Then Mr. Rohn I suggest you not do that anymore"*. If what you are doing is not allowing you to live the life you are deserving of I suggest you not do that anymore. Very simple. Very powerful. Very true.

When you decide to trade those goals and that plan for the commitment become what you are deserving of, then everything begins to change. Most importantly you will begin to change. If you decide to change it will all change for you. Here is the absolute for us all. We are getting what we are getting by doing what we are doing. In order to have something different we must do something different. Goals are the purposeful seeds of the mind and your plan is the nourishment that will allow it to grow. If we don't plant the seeds of promise and simply allow the winds to blow, the seeds that will take over are the weeds.

Once you have set the compass to where you want to go and who you want to become, the first critical step is to begin the research. Research is a key component to how well your journey will go and how much time it will take to get there. The intention of this stage is to find out all that you can about what you need to accomplish and who you need to become in order to have what you are deserving of. You have to go searching in order to find. Be grateful that you are beginning this quest during this time in history. There is so much at our fingertips today that simply did not exist 20 years ago. The advent of the Internet has brought about such an incredible collection of knowledge and answers that will speed along your process. There are experts and videos and websites that will open doors for you to continue along your journey.

It is important to know and accept that it is immensely important for you to be prepared to be a good student along the way. No degree was ever awarded for cutting class. Also, one of the great advantages of living today is that most everything you want to learn or become has been done before. Anthony Robbins made his millions telling people to find out what works and to do that. Great philosophy. You can take out a machete and try and carve your way through the forest or you can look for the path well travelled and walk there. All of the accomplishments of mankind. All of the pitfalls and mistakes and failures have been documented in libraries and now exist on the Internet of what you will encounter and need to learn. There are rare times when you may have to strike out on your own but key here is rarely.

Growing up the way I did I developed a chip on my shoulder early on that I didn't need anyone's help. I was angry and believed I should be smart enough to figure this out on my own. That attitude caused me to fall down a lot and skin my knee. In my mid-twenties when I finally let that wall down and started to seek out what I could learn from others everything began to change. Today I am absolutely fascinated by what is available to us all.

Think about this for just a moment. A person will take the entire sum total of their knowledge and experience over a lifetime and write it all down in a book and share all that knowledge with you for just a few dollars. It is one of the great deals of life. One final note on the research portion of your journey. Don't rush this. I know and understand that you are eager to set about the business of getting to your destination but rushing the process of research will invariably slow down your journey and provide for more unnecessary pitfalls. The structure of your research will be well laid out in the exercise from the end of this chapter. Take your time with this and do your very best work. Leave no stone unturned.

Regardless of where you are in life at this moment it's important to not get faked out by age. There are so many different parts of life that we will pass through. From infancy through our toddler years into childhood, teenage angst and our adult years all bring their own unique qualities and challenges. I remember like it was yesterday that I was the kid. For the longest time I was referred to as just that. The kid. I was 16 when I began working full time. 18 when I owned my first business. 21 when I landed a job in sales with a fortune 500 company. And so it went. Somewhere between those days and today it shifted. I was "the old guy" getting into radio at 28. Beyond most in years when I started a career in personal development and I certainly didn't fit the mold when I was blessed with a son at 49 and daughter at 53.

Here is what I have come to know. Age has little to do with the day unless you allow the cloud of perception to steal away the experience and ultimately your potential. A client commented one day that she was "46" and felt near the end of the line to be getting into her field. The number has nothing to do with it. Your perspective has everything. Here is what I know. She has 46 years experience to invest into the next great idea and endeavor. Here is what she also has. Likely close to 50 more years to ply her trade and live her life. That's where the focus must lie. On what lies ahead not what has passed. Here is a question that should put this all into context. *"Is a day any more valuable at age 46 than it is at 86"?* I expect we get the same 24 hours in a day no matter when they come along in life. Make the note to have the best days you can.

Harland Sanders was 65 when he struck out with 11 herbs and spices to start up his little venture called Kentucky Fried Chicken. At the time all he had was 11 herbs and spices and a burning belief that everyone would love what he had created. In the early going he lived in his car and went from restaurant to restaurant offering up his recipe in exchange for a few pennies an order for those who tried it. He knocked on 1007 doors before he heard his first yes. Here's what all of this means. Never allow the world to steal away your next dream because of a number.

As you work to put together your plan one of the most often overlooked tools of success are those who have come before. The mentors. Enlisting the help of a mentor can cut the time it takes to reach your destination more than you could imagine. Here is what you are to do. Seek out the most powerful and most successful person in your chosen field and ask them for advice. How's that for bold? Actually it may be the simplest thing you've ever done. Once you're able to spend some time with a mentor, you'll realize by seeing them as human how attainable your goal really is. Also, the information a mentor will be able to provide is invaluable.

Mike Cooper was my mentor in radio and, in a very significant way, the reason I'm where I am today. My dream since I was a child was to work in radio. After listening to all the reasons that the odds were stacked against me, I finally made a phone call at age 28 and needed all the help that I could get. In the beginning, my goal was to one day work a daytime shift and make enough money to support my family. I thought that if I could do that, my life would be fulfilled. Two years after getting my first job in radio, I had a conversation that changed my life. At a barbecue, a friend of mine was asking about my new job. The conversation led to talking about an announcer who I thought was the best of the best. When I mentioned the host's name he said, *"I know him. Actually, I don't really know him, but my wife's brother works with him. He's in the sports department. Why don't I set it up and you can call him?"*

"Sure," I thought, *"that's not likely to happen".*

That's exactly what happened.

Making the call was nerve-wracking. I was surprised when he was so gracious on the phone and invited me to come down and sit in on his show. He took me through the do's and don'ts of the business. He invited me out for a beer after the show, and he was the one who made me believe. Something remarkable happens when you have the chance to meet face to face with people we idolize. They become real. He taught me that less is more and that I should strive to become the listener's friend. He also taught me to never, never go on the air unprepared. Amateurs wing it, he said; professionals never take that chance. His experience of decades was offered up freely. What I learned from Mike was invaluable. It changed the course of my career.

When I left him that night to drive the hour or so north to my hometown, my entire mission statement had changed. I no longer was satisfied with the prospect of one day being able to support my family with my job as a radio announcer. In hindsight, I realize that my initial goal was, in effect, to settle. My goal after that first meeting was to strive to the top and be one of those people who made it. Thanks to my friend who gave me the courage to make that call, I did make it to the No. 1 radio station in the country. Looking back, I can't help but wonder where I would have ended up had it not been for his help.

There's something magical about those who have made it. They remember the days when the mountain ahead seemed so daunting. Most will inherently want to help others facing the same mountain. It is also true that when someone comes to them looking for advice, they can tell whether the person has genuine passion or not. Passion is a very tangible commodity.

If you're questioning whether it will happen for you, the answer is *"not every time."* There are those at the top who won't be so gracious and helpful. You simply have to accept this and move on to the next person. I believe however that the majority will be more than willing to help out. The reality is that very few people at the top are approached. It's like the beautiful woman who sits home alone on a Saturday night. You would think she'd be asked out constantly. The truth is, few *"nice guys"* can muster the courage to ask her out, so she sits home alone. The same holds true for the mentors out there waiting for your call.

Those who have made it will admire your drive and conviction. There are three reasons that they're likely to help. First and foremost, they're just people, like anyone else. While you and many others idolize them, they generally don't see themselves that way. Second, they probably came up through the ranks and recall what that was like. No one starts at the top. They can empathize with you and probably wish they'd had someone to turn to for advice and guidance themselves or perhaps they did. Finally, they will be flattered. For most, it's a humbling experience to be looked up to.

I want you to know and believe that this process is totally possible and likely for you. One of the aspects of this process to focus on is the life experience that you have now. Its common for us to dismiss events or skills we have experienced and learned during our lives as being completely inconsequential and of no value to our current journey. It may seem that way but nothing could be further from the truth. Everything in life happens for a reason. Every thought we have, every action we take, every beat of our heart prepares us for the next challenge and the view over the ridge of the next mountain. I am fascinated every day at the realization of what I have been through and what I have done in the past that has assisted in what I am doing right now.

My time living on the streets provided the incredible perspective of light and dark that validates my work as a speaker and coach. It has all added experience and knowledge and had an impact. My jobs in sales and radio and television and stocking shelves during the midnight shift at a grocery store helped form who I am and gave me a new depth. The knowledge you have today and the experiences that were part of your yesterday will bring forward more to your current journey than you could imagine. Know that all that you have done in the past will help you along the way to where you are going.

While putting together your plan, approach this as your job. This will be exciting and a bit scary but make no mistake you are going to have to take this seriously. With that in mind it is important to commit to the process of putting your plan together on a daily basis. Take action everyday. Set the goal to do something each day that will allow you to move forward.

I remember a great piece of philosophy I was given years ago when I first began writing. I was in radio and had begun writing a newspaper column. I loved doing it but felt that I was not up to the level of some of the other writers I enjoyed reading. One night after my show my wife and I went out to dinner with one of my guests who was a great fiction writer. Over dinner I shared my story with him and asked if he had any advice he could share that could help me become a better writer. *"Yes I do"* he said. *"Write every day"*. He went on to explain that the only way to become a better writer was to write when you have great ideas. To write when you have nothing to say. To write when you are tired and uninspired, when you are sick and overwhelmed. I took up his advice and have written almost every day since. I can't tell you just how important that advice is. If you want to get better at anything, commit to doing what is necessary and do it every day. When you are working on this plan or roadmap that will take you from where you are to where you deserve to be, take it seriously. Work on your plan every day.

Also when putting this plan together you may be required to make sacrifices along the way. It is possible that it may not happen but be prepared for the possibility. Just as the statement *"you get what you pay for"* is so absolute and true, the same applies to this process. You must be prepared to pay for what it is you hope to reap. When working on your plan be brutally honest with yourself. If you expect you will need to cut back in certain areas or invest a set amount of time to make it happen be honest and prepare and plan for it. After all, getting to where you want to go and becoming the person you deserve to be will certainly be worth it. The price you will pay is nothing compared to what you will become and the life experiences that will come from it.

One final piece of advice moving forward came to me a number of years ago and I consider it to be one of the most important pieces of personal philosophy I have ever heard. In a large way it is responsible for my being where I am today. John Stockdale was the highest-ranking officer held in the POW camps during the Viet Nam war. When the war ended and the camp liberated he was freed and came back to the U.S. Shortly after he was interviewed and what was revealed was astounding. The interviewer asked John Stockdale how it was that he survived such horrific conditions over 8 years when almost all others held in the Hanoi Hilton died. He said *"That's easy. They were the optimists"*. Somewhat taken aback the interviewer said, *"But didn't you need to be optimistic to survive"?* Mr. Stockdale replied, *"Of course but what happened was that they would say, we all need to hang on; and they were at deaths door everyday. Hang on, they would say and we'll be home by Christmas. Then Christmas would come and go. Then they would say don't die, we'll make it out by Easter and Easter would come and go, then one of the guys would say that he would be home to kiss his boy on his 9th birthday. The days came and the days went and over time it broke their spirit so bad they died. They lost their lives"*. John Stockdale went on to say that *"the moment I was captured I made the decision that I didn't know how and I didn't know when but I absolutely knew that one day I would be free"*. *"And that"* he said is what saved his life.

I refer to this in lectures and programs all the time. It's what I call the *"Stockdale Paradox"* and it is the absolute truth when setting out to achieve any goal. It is normal that we will set a timeline and estimate when we will achieve our goal. What you must know and accept is that you are not psychic. Not one of us can know with certainty exactly when our goal will show up. Do this. Commit to achieving your vision in life and then accept this statement. *"I don't know how and I don't know when but I absolutely know that one day I will achieve this. I will continue to do all that is in my power each and every day to move forward"*. That is the magic that propels the human spirit forward to achieve anything it sets out to do.

Exercise-The Plan

This is where the separation from dreams to reality begins. This is the first step in the transition from thought to substance. This exercise will provide for you the advantage of beginning this process and moving towards your goal with a plan. As with any major project, organization from the beginning is one of the most important aspects.

There will be 4 sections to your plan. They will include:

- o   Research

- o   Decision-bridge or cliff

o Transition activities

o Completion

The following questions will ultimately provide the answers that will allow for the creation of your plan. Be as detailed as possible and take as much time necessary to complete you're the questions below and create your plan. Following these questions, there will be a section to record your detailed answers followed by an activity tracking form that will allow you to detail action steps identified and completed.

-1 Vision

Once you have defined what you want to become and to achieve, fill out the promissory note below.

I _____ have decided that I am going to spend the rest of my life_____

_____

_____

_____

_____ I am 100% committed to making this happen and will not stop until I achieve it. I *WILL* be one of the lucky ones who can say that "I am living the life I designed"

Where can I research what is required to achieve my goal?

- o   -
- o   -
- o   -
- o   -
- o   -

What changes will be necessary in my life in order to make this happen

- o   Career
- o   Family responsibilities
- o   Available time for new venture
- o   Financial considerations
- o   Personal support

What will you need to accomplish to achieve your goal?

- o   Qualifications necessary

- o   Education
  - o   What and where

- o   Practical experience

- o   Financial consideration
  - o   Savings
  - o   Skills you have to earn money to transition through the process
  - o   Altering lifestyle to reduce expenses through the process

- o Research the various options for earning money doing what you love (job)

- o Find a mentor(s)
  - o Make a list of who is doing what you have identified and contact them asking for advice.

Once your research is complete in each of these areas, it's time for you to sit down and begin to put together a master plan. Again, make certain you don't make the mistake of trusting any of this to memory. The power of the written goal is that it becomes a personal contract with you. This not only will give you a firm foundation but also will serve as a major motivator to detail your progress from day to day.

As with all plans, it's imperative that you project dates when you expect a particular aspect of your plan will be completed. This will allow you to forecast the activity necessary to achieve each element of the plan. The one caveat to this however is The Stockdale Paradox. Of greater importance than creating a timeline is the realization and acceptance that ultimately *"you won't know how and you won't know when but if you don't stop"* you will without question reach your goal of living the life you were meant to.

Putting together a master plan may at first appear daunting, but it's actually quite a simple process. In essence what a master plan is, is a detailed list of all the necessary steps in the right chronological order necessary to achieve your goal. The more detailed your list, the better your progress will be.

Master plan:

From your research collected above it is now time to organize your plan in chronological order. The framework of your plan will begin where you are at this moment in time and will culminate where you are living the life you have designed.

Goal

_____

_____

_____

_____

_____

Research timeline

_____

_____

_____

Mentor

_____

_____

_____

_____

Skill development –education and practical experience

_____

_____

_____

_____

Income production-(choose how you will earn a living doing what you love)

_____

_____

_____

_____

_____

Decision-bridge or cliff

_____

_____

_____

_____

Lifestyle adjustments

_____

_____

_____

_____

Transitional income (if required)

_____

_____

_____

_____

_____

Once you have completed the exercise above, it is now time to begin to

arrange all actions and activities in chronological order. Take your time to

complete your vision template. This will allow you to bring structure and

organization to the journey you are about to embark on. Use the space

provided below to create the step-by-step structure required to achieve

your goal.

Action Tracker

Action	Est/time	Steps Required	Completed

_____

_____

_____

_____

_____

_____

_____

_____

_____

_____

_____

_____

_____

Take your time and make certain to use the tracking form above. It will allow you to see your progress which is essential in providing the continued motivation to see the process through to completion. This will allow you to bring structure and organization to the journey you are about to embark on. Once your plan is completed, next you will learn perhaps the most important element of this entire process.

11

The Swoosh

At this point all the thought and all the philosophy and all the best intentions in the world will do nothing to allow you to lead the life you are so deserving to lead without the next step. The final element in the process to breathe life into your dreams and to be one of those authentic souls who is "Looking forward to Monday's" can be found in the following story. One of the great examples and the story of the magic of achieving hopes and goals and dreams can be traced back to a fledgling company in 1971 that were looking for a logo. At the time a young graphic design student was retained from Portland University. She had met the businessman while he was teaching accounting classes at the university. She was hired on for $2. an hour and she presented several designs before one was finally agreed upon. When the work was done she submitted her invoice for $35. Today you know her work because of the likes of Michael Jordan, LeBron James, Andre Agassi, Maria Sharapova, Venus and Serena Williams and many more. The company takes it name from the Greek goddess of victory, Nike. This simple swoosh would go on and be pared with a slogan that may be one of the greatest philosophies of personal growth ever penned. *Just do it!*

I am sitting here with only a paragraph written on the most important step in this process of becoming what you are deserving of. That is to know why you are here and who you are about to become. To become someone who is authentic. Someone who knows his or her why in life. Someone who has designed their own life and is ready to pull it off. I am struggling with whether to write pages and pages with all the reasons and philosophy and stories and urging to get you to take this final step. To do this. To, as Nike says, *"just do it"*. I have decided to let this be your own urging. I will simply ask this. How bad do you want it? How much will it mean to you to wake up every morning knowing that you have figured this out and you are no longer simply trading life for money? How bad do you want to avoid those last days on earth when you sit and wonder what your life was all about? If you want this. If you really, really want this, know that more than anything in the world I want this for you and believe with everything inside of me that you can do it. Take this last step then. Shrug off the blanket of doubt and just do it! God's speed.

There are a few points I wanted to finish up with. Some final pieces of the puzzle that I wanted to leave you with before you set to the process of designing your own life. The first is a certain responsibility I would like you to consider from the outset. As you are about to embark on a truly remarkable journey that will leave you filled up and satisfied and full of passion, I would like you to consider sharing all that you will achieve with others. Set the goal to live your life for a cause greater than your own. I'm not sure what that will be or what it will look like or who it will touch but I do know that to those who are given much, much is expected. There are so many millions of people around the world who look across the ocean at us and wonder what it must be like to have so much opportunity. So much hope. So much promise. I ask that you take what you have learned going through this and pay it forward. Philanthropy and paying forward the blessings of life truly is one of the most selfish acts once tasted. Those who receive without question gain but those who give are filled up in ways that can only be understood when experienced. Take your experience then and share it with the world and with those who would dream for the life you are about to have.

One last point I would like to leave you with is to ask you to *"Guard well the flame"*. When discovering your passion and vision in life is in its infancy I would like you to make a promise to yourself that you will keep this to yourself. I understand that it is human nature when we have an idea or get excited about the prospect of something new that we want to tell our family and friends and everyone. I suggest you not do that and here is why. The reason that most people today are not following their heart is because they shared their ideas with the world in the early going and the world immediately warned of all the pitfalls of the venture. Again, it is doubt that pushes all goals off into the distance. Doubt that was created by the intake of information from the world around us. Believing we "can't" is not something we were born with. It was something that was taught to us by the world.

I often relate the analogy in seminars of a character on a television show called Survivorman. The premise of the show is that he goes out and lives in the wild for 7 days with no food or shelter or protection. As the sun goes down he sets about the business of starting a fire to protect himself from predators and to stay warm. This is normally done by rubbing sticks together or sparking a flint. He works and works and works until finally a tiny spark causes a bit of smoke to come up from the dried grass. He cups his hands and blows on it ever so gently until a tiny flame begins to form. This reminds me of the process of going after your dreams. This is the stage in the early going when it has been defined and is in its infancy. At this point if we share it with the world, the world more than likely will come along and blow it out. When that happens, the sad reality is that we may never try and light the fire again. Do this then. When your vision and passion are in the early stages tell no one. Cup your hands around it and protect it with all you have. Wait until the flame is burning brightly before you share it with the world. Once it becomes a large fire it is all but impossible to blow out.

This book was not written to entertain you. Millions of great books are written and read every day. The sad reality is that they fail to create substantive change in the lives of the reader. The information may be first class, however the structure is missing as to how to implement in practical terms what is necessary to create the change the reader was seeking in the first place.

There is one final aspect of this process to consider. That is to enjoy the journey; but first the story of the barefoot boys.

The Barefoot Boys

The following is a reprint of a news story I came across a number of years ago. I was invited to speak to the staff of The Globe and Mail and while waiting in the green room to take the stage, I came across this story in their own newspaper. It is one of the most inspiring stories I ever read and is a fantastic example of what we are all capable of.

The IITs are 16 separate engineering colleges spread across India which, taken together, are perhaps the most elite educational institutions in the world. More than 500,000 students wrote the entrance exam this year. Just 8,000 were admitted. That is an acceptance rate of less than two per cent, lower than that of, for example, Harvard University, or Oxford. An IIT degree is a passport to wealth and respect; to a life a million miles from the low-roofed porch where Mr. Yadav studied by lantern light, a couple of water buffalo tied to a peg near his feet.

But no one in Rashulpur, a village of cowherds and feudal farm labor, has ever gone to college. No one has ever met an engineer. And no one knew what the IIT was, when Mr. Yadav came home that day with the news.

"I didn't know what it meant, but when I found out, I felt like my dream had been achieved," his mother, Radhika said, surveying her shy and lanky son with bemused pride. "I knew even if I had to starve, I would teach my children. When I saw educated people I wanted my children to be like them - when I saw how they dressed, how they lived."

Mr. Yadav, 18, wrote the IIT entrance exam in May, alongside 29 students who had joined him in an extraordinary academic endeavor. They are called the Super 30, and they are teenagers from the most marginal families in some of the most marginal corners of India.

Each year 30 students, as impoverished as they are promising, are recruited by a rumpled, near-fanatical math teacher named Anand Kumar. Over the course of seven months, he tutors, teaches, mentors, badgers and crams as much as he can into their thirsty brains in preparation for the IIT exam. He has run Super 30 for eight years, and in three of those years, all 30 have made it in. This year, 26, including Mr. Yadav, made the cut. These are statistics unmatched by the most elite of the IIT-entrance coaching institutes anywhere in India.

"I want to show that if you have will power, even in Bihar, you don't need infrastructure or money," said Mr. Kumar. "You just need devoted teachers."

He and his ramshackle school are a source of both pride and curiosity in India - the pass rates of his Super 30 make headlines every year. But beyond the novelty value of the barefoot boys (they are almost all boys) who are vaulted into the country's elite, the furor around Super 30 points to a growing crisis in Indian education.

The roaring economy has created a desperate thirst for skilled graduates. But there is massive shortage of accredited educational institutions to teach them. India's economic reforms, which eased the choke hold of bureaucracy and corruption, kicked off this era of growth 15 years ago. But those reforms have yet to be applied to education. There are near-insurmountable bureaucratic obstacles to opening a new accredited institution. Instead, thousands of unaccredited schools have sprung up, offering education of wildly varying quality, luring students who hope that employers hungry for engineers or business graduates won't scrutinize their credentials too closely.

India's Human Resource and Development Minister, Kapil Sibal, recently told journalists that the country needed 1,500 new universities just to keep pace with demand. But he has resisted calls to allow the development of private institutions, while doing nothing to ease the path for public schools to expand.

Thus the IITs become ever more exclusive. Mr. Kumar, 39, did not attend an IIT himself. He grew up in the Bihari capital of Patna, the son of a low-caste clerk in the postal bureau, and was at best bound for a similar job himself.

But Mr. Kumar proved to have a rare brilliance with math, a genius that shone even in the dire public schools he attended, and he won a place at Cambridge University in 1994. His family scrambled to figure out a way to finance his studies, but before he could leave for England, his father died suddenly. It fell to his mother and Mr. Kumar to support the family; the dream of Cambridge was shelved and instead she made pappadums and he sold them from a bicycle. "This was our only source of survival," he recalled, his face twisting at the memory.

Mr. Kumar was taken on by a professor at Patna University who caught wind of his rare abilities. Before long he was publishing in international mathematics journals. He began tutoring other students - poor kids like he was. Their numbers grew quickly, and in 2002 he formalized his tutoring into a school.

His classes were free in the beginning, but eventually he asked students to pay a fee of 500 rupees - about $11 - for the year, so that he could afford to run the school full-time. Most agreed, but one of the brightest students asked if he could pay in installments. Puzzled, Mr. Kumar asked him why. The boy said it would take his father some time to scrape together the money. Mr. Kumar followed the child home that night and discovered that he was working in domestic service, sleeping under a stairwell and studying in patches of light he could find at night.

Mr. Kumar resolved to gather up 30 - as many as he could house and feed - of the best and poorest students and train them for the IIT.

For the rest of the school, he would teach middle- and upper-class kids for 5,000 rupees ($110) per course per year - far lower than the usual elite tuition rates and just enough that he would break even, running Super 30.

More than half his first Super 30 students won places at the IIT - and not everyone was happy about it. Soon he had death threats from gangsters, contract killers hired by what he calls the "coaching mafia," owners of for-profit tuition centers who didn't like his low prices or his success rates. The police assigned him two full-time bodyguards.

Mr. Kumar teaches in a huge tin-roofed, dirt-floored shed down an alley choked with trash, stray cows and sewage. A dozen ceiling fans do nothing to cut the soupy heat. The students - about 150, on a typical morning, a dozen of them girls - sit on rough wood benches and place their notebooks, limp in the humidity, on planks in front of them. Mr. Kumar wears a screechy lapel microphone, but hardly needs it: his wild excitement for quadratic equations has him yelling through half the lesson. He intersperses the math with motivational sermons, reminding his students that their background does not matter, that they are smart enough for any test, that all they need is to work and believe they can do it.

Mr. Kumar expects total commitment. "Don't sleep!" he exhorts them, mopping his face with a handkerchief. "Work hard! In 24 hours, study 14 or 16. No TV! No newspapers, no sports, no games! Just study, study, study!"

Mr. Yadav - who is so thin it seems improbable his neck can hold a brain so crammed with knowledge - began his studies at the tumbledown village school. "The building wasn't good, but the teachers showed up."

He tried to write the IIT exam on his own a year ago, but failed it. Then he read about Super30 in the newspaper, and wrote the entry test to join Mr. Kumar's small group. "I needed a good guide who could work with me, but it was not possible if I had to pay," he said. As beaming family members clustered three-deep around him, he allowed himself a small smile. "It feels good to be in."

The cost of attending an IIT is about $4,500 a year, minimal compared to say the Massachusetts Institute of Technology, but wildly beyond Mr. Yadav's family's means. Mr. Kumar has negotiated with a bank to secure him a loan, as he must do every year for his Super 30 students.

Mr. Yadav already knows what he will do with his first paycheque from the job he lands with his IIT degree: return to Vaishali. "The first thing I will spend money on is to build a school, a really good school, for people of my background," he said. "After completing [a degree from IIT] I will have powers to help poor people like myself - I will do things for my village and my state."

Here is my greatest hope of sharing this final story with you. That you see. That you truly see and accept without reservation that you have everything inside of you to become anything you imagined. Now on to the final chapter in this process.

12

Enjoy the journey

"It is good to have an end to journey toward; but it is the journey that matters in the end."

Ursula K. LeGuin

L ife moves so quickly that we forget to look out the window, to feel the wind in our face and enjoy the ride. You're about to embark on one of the most amazing trips of your life; don't miss it. What happens far too often is that we spend too much time fixated on the destination and miss out on the most rewarding part of life: the journey.

Getting from here to there will provide more of a roller coaster of emotions and memories than you may ever have the chance to experience again. How you approach the journey is about choice. Allow yourself to rekindle the feelings that you had as a child when you explored for the first time. Remember how it felt when you were able to walk to the store all by yourself for the first time.

We all still have that child inside us. The reason we don't get to see him or her now is that we've been told to grow up and act our age. Rekindling the emotions of your youth doesn't make you a child. It gives you the ability to reclaim the courage to dream. If being an adult means not living with a sense of wonder and excitement, I would suggest that being "grown up" is sad existence.

You're going to want to look back and remember these days. Take lots of pictures of what's happening as you journey down this road. What kind of car were you driving when you began? Where were you living at the time? Who were the people you were friends with? What work did you do to get you through these times, and who were the people you worked with? What did your life look like when you came to terms with what your true passion was?

Your journey is very much like going fishing. It's not just about pulling the big one into the boat. It's about everything that's involved in getting to the point when you can claim the prize. Success is about much more than just hooking a fish and pulling it in. If this were the case, fishermen would be content to go to a stocked fish pond, cast their lines and have someone put the hook in the fishes' mouth.

It's not about just that. It was never about that.. It's about shopping for that perfect rod and reel. It's about buying the fishing magazines and reading up on techniques and new products. It's about trying to discover that secret hole you heard about where "they're bitin' ". It's about loading the car and hooking up the boat, about driving hours north or south, about packing a cooler, about looking for bait, about swatting the insects or ducking a storm. It's about fondly recalling the story of the "big one" that got away. It's about getting skunked and coming right back the next week or the next month to try it all over again. And it's about being able to stand back and admire that trophy you were finally able to put on the wall. While taking the steps to reach your personal goal, don't forget to enjoy the ride. You'll never pass this way again.

"Life is just a collection of memories

of our journey through life."

The coming days and months invested in achieving your dream will be the most exciting, rewarding, challenging and memorable of your life. These will be the days you will fondly recall when you decided to finally take control of your life and do what you love rather than what society had conditioned you to do. How you deal with this time is simply a question of *"mental control."* If you choose to view it as drudgery, every day will be long and hard and difficult. If, on the other hand, you choose to attack every day with excitement and anticipation, your journey will give birth to memories that you'll cherish for years to come.

Now that you have decided to embark on this journey, smile quietly to yourself. You are about to go through the most profound change imaginable as you begin to create your life of passion and purpose. I was driving home from delivering a seminar one day and a song came on the radio. It brought tears to my eyes. The words summed up how I felt about how my life has turned out.

266

"Did you ever hear about a frog who dreamed of being a king ... and then became one? Well, except for the names and a few other changes, when you talk about me, the story's the same one."

Neil Diamond

With everything inside of me, this is my greatest wish for you. That you do what it takes to find the passion that beats inside of you and to breathe life into it. I know and believe that you will be one of those extraordinary souls who will wake up one day very soon and to say. *"I'm looking forward to Monday".*

THE END

..........................YOUR NEW BEGINNING

To contact Randy

rtaylor@taylormadeleadership.com

Be well,

Randy Taylor

Randy Taylor-Bio

Randy Taylor is one of the bright new lights in the world of personal growth and leadership. Having escaped poverty, parent alcoholism and life on the streets Randy was able to overcome incredible odds. Beginning at age 28 he was able to reach the very top in Canadian broadcasting as the drive home talk show host of CFRB 1010 and as the host of Summit of Life on Global Television. His level of expertise has won him several national broadcast awards.

Nine years ago Randy left broadcasting to form Taylormadeleadership. Through his own personal experience and study for over thirty years he has developed a dynamic new leadership philosophy called "The Winner Within". This program along with 3 other dynamic coaching programs have has recently received national accreditation from the largest financial services company in Canada. He is quickly gaining notoriety among some of the top corporations and associations in North America. His client list includes Investors Group, Bell Canada, Motorola, Aim Trimark, Xerox, ReMax Realty, Petro Canada, Kraft Foods, The Globe and Mail, The Government of Canada, London Life, Brookfield Homes, Toronto Youth Services and many more.

To Book Randy Taylor to speak at your next conference or in-house event, please contact;

seminars@taylormadeleadership.com

or visit our website

www.taylormadeleadership.com